Gun Fights, Ghosts and Goannas

A Solo Motorcycle Tour of Queensland

Gary Wood

 A catalogue record for this book is available from the National Library of Australia

Copyright © 2024 by Gary Wood

All rights reserved, no part of this book may be reproduced or used in any manner including the right to reproduce this book or portions thereof in any form without the written permission of the copyright owner.

This book is non-fiction.

Publisher:
Digital Swaggie Publishing
Email: gary@digitalswaggie.com.au
http://digitalswaggie.com.au

National Library of Australia Prepublication Data Service

Author: Gary Wood

Title: **Gun Fights, Ghosts and Goannas**
  A Solo Motorcycle Tour of Queensland

Genre: Travel and Adventure

ISBN: 978-1-7635631-0-0 (print)
ISBN: 978-1-7635631-2-4 (hardcover)
ISBN: 978-1-7635631-1-7 (ebook)

Table of Contents

Prologue 3

Chapter 1: I Dream a Dream 5

Chapter 2: Sitting at the dock of a bay 9

Chapter 3: Twisting the Throttle 18

Chapter 4: Life on the road 31

Chapter 5: Hunting Ghosts 41

Chapter 6: The True Story of Waltzing Matilda 48

Chapter 7: Land of Dinosaurs 58

Chapter 8: Gunslingers and Opal Miners 64

Chapter 9: My Religious Experience 85

Chapter 10: The Birth of Australian Democracy 93

Chapter 11: International Chicken Racing 98

Chapter 12: Mastering the Wilderness Way 103

Chapter 13: Murderous Conflict 111

Chapter 14: Cattle Country 116

Chapter 15: Captain Starlight Was Here 122

Chapter 16: Fishing in the Outback 132

Chapter 17: Riding the Scenic Rim 142

Chapter 18: From Rustic to Rush Hour -
the Gold Coast Experience 160

Chapter 19: Cafe Racing 174

Chapter 20: The Sunshine Coast 182

Chapter 21: Who was Harry and why did he build this hut? ...190

Chapter 22: Chasing the Rainbow Serpent 196

Chapter 23: Riding the Great Sandy Strait 204

Chapter 24: How does a polar bear promote rum? 211

Chapter 24: Lieutenant James Cook RN was here 1770 217

Chapter 25: Back in the Tropics 228

Chapter 26: North Queensland's first deepwater port 232

Chapter 27: Back to the Outback 247

Chapter 28: The quirkiest pub in the outback 251

Chapter 29: Gold Fever 255

Chapter 30: Back in Townsville 274

Prologue

It was a humid summer night, the air thick with moisture, sweat forming on the back of my neck when I hatched a plan to ride a motorcycle around Queensland. There were a few problems to overcome, like not owning a bike and not having a license to ride one. All I knew for sure was that life was going in the wrong direction, and something had to change. Work satisfaction was at an all-time low and I kept having this vision of inserting a stapler up the boss's arse, to show him what I thought of micro-management. But it's more than individual actions, we all seem to be working in a drone-like environment where sensibility has gone out the window, and it's more important to have a gender pronoun than to be a productive, cooperative worker. A motorcycle trip seemed like a good idea at the time and a solution to my quickly declining mental health.

Inspired by a rerun of *City Slicker* and Curly's one-finger salute to the secret of life, I acquired the resources, learnt to ride a motorcycle again, and set off for a solo 30-day camping tour around Queensland. I went searching for a different view of the world—one with traditional values of mateship and hard work, the old fun-loving larrikin Australia.

Gun Fights, Ghosts and Goannas is a travel journal about riding a motorcycle around Queensland, meeting locals, learning the history of the place, and discovering the secrets of life along the way. I hope this book inspires you to get on the road, get away from your nine-to-five job, and appreciate the beauty in life before it's too late. Along the way, I guarantee you will experience the "WOW Factors" and "Moments" that take your breath away and make you feel alive.

Motorcycles can't by themselves build your resilience or change your mindset; it's the people you meet, the adversity you overcome, and the self-reliance you develop along the journey that does that. A motorcycle is the vehicle that takes you on that journey. If you get on your bike and twist the throttle, it won't be long until you know what Curly meant when he raised his finger.

Chapter 1
It Started with a Dream

This book is about adventure motorcycle riding, middle age, and chicken racing, but most of all, it's about adventure and what it means to be an adventurer. Over two years, I rode 20,000 kilometres around Queensland. During this time I dodged giant snakes, suicidal kangaroos, ghosts, and tornadoes. I prepared for a gunfight in an opal mining town and uncovered the real story behind the song "Waltzing Matilda" and the old swaggie murdered at an outback billabong. Along the way, I discovered the quintessential Australian culture and understood where that brash, confident country the world once knew came from. Australia had a vibrant, fresh culture of hardworking, beer-drinking larrikins, genuine people who you could rely on when times were tough. Deep down I wanted to find out if those people still existed out there somewhere out there in the Outback. I always wondered why it is called the Outback, perhaps I'll find out.

But the essence of this book is about travelling through Queensland on a motorcycle, taking time to realise what's important in life and realising that our time on Earth is limited. It's about finding those little things on our journeys that inspire and motivate us, and it's about how sometimes the destination is important, but the journey provides the experiences that change our lives.

I've heard it said that riding a motorcycle is a form of therapy, that spending time in one's thoughts, working through diversity, and meeting new people is a way of resetting one's perspective.

After 42 years of work, I found it hard to focus on my career aspirations anymore, and my job was whittling my life away, hour by hour. The politics and lack of integrity in many workplaces today are unbearable. I'd gotten to the point in my life and career where there were no more surprises, no excitement. It was just a constant battle not to jam a stapler up some woke bastard's arse, just for the satisfaction of doing it and to release that built-up aggression and frustration that comes with people telling you their fucking pronouns.

I knew I needed a circuit breaker; I needed to shift my thinking and change my mindset. There was a feeling of impending doom that just seemed to creep up on me like the rolling fog of the Yorkshire countryside. Was this what life is all about from now on? I thought to myself, a nine-to-five drudgery, day after day watching life from behind a window as it slowly passes by. Surely, there was more to life than working to pay a mortgage, buy a car, and take two weeks of holidays a year?

The thin veil that masks reality and keeps us working nine to five was starting to fall away for me, I looked out of the window and saw a bird fly past and out to sea. I wonder if the bird works nine to five. Sure, battery hens do, but we humans have created that reality for them, just like we have created this one for ourselves.

That night, lying back in my hammock contemplating the meaning of life, a song came through my speaker, one I hadn't heard since my late 20s. It was "Dock of the Bay" by Ottis Redding and it brought back the dream I once had of riding a motorcycle around Australia.

But somehow it seemed like more than a dream; it was almost like the road was calling me to make this happen. If motorcycle riding is therapy, I may need some of that to reset my mind.

It's interesting how music can take you back to another time and bring back not just memories, but whole experiences, feelings, and emotions, almost as if you were back there once more. So real, you can smell the hops in the beer you were drinking, taste the slight essence of sugar, and feel the bubbles of CO_2 tickle your mouth as the beer effortlessly slides down your throat. Then, moments later, the hit of energy from the sugar. We sometimes forget all of this, with our minds focused on things that don't matter in the end.

Once we had dreams and goals, but somewhere in this Orwellian world, we became bland servants of an unseen master. For many, including myself, a world without dreams is a living hell.

I started thinking about dreams, and the difference between a dream and a bucket list item or a goal. I concluded that a dream is like a happy thought, a will-o'-the-wisp, a fleeting wisp of light. A dream feels good, and you can get lost in the romanticism of possibilities. A bucket list item is the next stage in the manifestation of the dream; this is where shit gets real, and you end up choosing one of the multitudes of possibilities open to you.

So many people have dreams that never go anywhere, I worry my dreams will go unfulfilled, and when I get too old, I will regret never having tried to achieve them. A life unfulfilled with regret is a living hell, this is what keeps me up at night. Then I thought the opposite of a dream is a nightmare; I wonder if many people suffer from nightmares. The thought that your life is slipping away so fast that there is very little time to achieve your dreams is a nightmare.

I'm uncertain if it was the red wine or the blues music playing, as I sat alone in my hammock on the outside patio, but something stirred inside me, like a spark. "I might be getting old," I thought to myself, "but I'm not fucking dead yet, there's still time."

Chapter 2
Sitting at the Dock of the Bay

I see myself, I'm riding down an isolated highway; it's hot and blustery. The tar-sealed road stretches beyond my vision. To my left is the most beautiful azure sea, in the distance, turbulent white caps, and on my right, a land of ochre dirt punctuated with little tufts of mottled green plants and dry taupe grasses to the horizon. I have a feeling of utter freedom. But the image is not clear; it's a hazy, washed-out version of reality.

This is a dream I've had before with endless possibilities, it fades away once my rational mind kicks in and tells me to wake up and be sensible. I've had this dream to ride a motorcycle around Australia. It would surface every five years from the age of 29. But I've been too busy with my studies or my career. Later, I rationalised that the kids were too small; what if I had an accident, who would look after them?

Then one night, listening to music, this dream surfaced again, but this time another thought accompanied it, my younger self sitting and listening to music at Fisherman's Wharf on the Gold Coast back in the 1980s. The music was "The Dock of the Bay" by Ottis Redding. Strangely enough, that song is about life drifting away; when I first heard it, I associated it with freedom of spirit.

Even though it brought back memories of freedom, it now had a different meaning. It could be a message from my past, put in place for this exact moment to remind me life can pass you by. Let's face it, that was 36 years ago and I'm still haunted by a dream of riding around Australia. So then and there, I made this dream a goal, taking my dream and putting a time frame to it. Now I am committed to making this goal happen. I decided I would start with Queensland and then ride each state until I finally got around Australia.

I got up and went to the lounge to tell my wife that I had made a goal to finally ride around Australia. She said again, what she had said the first time I mentioned when I met her in a bar near the university we were both studying at. "I said, I'm not riding with you around Australia," "You're not coming, I responded this is my dream, maybe you should get one of your own." So after a couple of days of silent treatment, my wife broke the silence. "Well, you have a bit of a problem, don't you," she said in a slightly condescending, sarcastic tone. "You don't have a motorcycle or a license."

Now, as much as I hate to admit it, she was right, but I wasn't going to let a mere technicality scuttle my dream and my goal. Having highlighted my situation, she had inadvertently and unconsciously provided a solution. I took that to mean, "Go out and buy yourself a motorcycle, darling."

The first step was to get my motorcycle license. Unfortunately, my New Zealand motorcycle license was no longer valid, so I had to enrol in a motorcycle riding course. However, once you have completed the course, you can't just get on your bike and go.

You have to wait three months, during this time you are meant to be supervised by a qualified rider.

The only person in our family who had a motorcycle license was my wife, she has only ever ridden bikes on her family's cattle property. When she went for her car license, the officer asked if she wanted her motorcycle and truck licenses, at the same time. And as if they were being given away with every glass of Chardonnay at the local pub, she accepted.

As a side note, her mother also got her articulated truck license at the same police station, even though she had never driven an articulated truck. Word to the wise: always be wary of articulated trucks on country roads in central Queensland.

So, here I am, having ridden motorbikes since I was six years old, being followed around Townsville by my qualified wife, who had no road riding experience. How humiliating. It would have been less humiliating if she hadn't mentioned it every day for the next three months and made a special note to tell all our friends she was supervising me on a bike.

Then, as if to rub salt in the wound, she put it on her Facebook page and to make sure all my friends knew, she even posted it to my timeline as well. I'm not even sure how she did that. I suspect teenage hackers may have helped.

Talking of teenaged hackers, my children even got into the action, threatening to share it on TikTok and Instagram, until I reminded them that I still paid for their mobile phones, the subject was quickly dropped and never mentioned again.

The license was the first obstacle in my grand plan to ride around Australia, starting with Queensland. The next obstacle was what type of motorcycle I should buy.

When you get your license in Queensland, you're not allowed to jump on a Ninja 1000 and ride into the sunset. You must ride what's called a LAMS bike, LAMS being a fit-sounding title. LAMS stands for Learner Approved Motorcycle Scheme. The LAMS program is designed so kids can't get big powerful bikes and kill themselves straight up; they must wait a couple of years before they can do that.

The decision to purchase a motorcycle was therefore restricted to those that fit the LAMS requirements. My choice of motorcycle also had to suit the rigorous conditions I would encounter riding around Queensland. To put this into perspective, riding around Queensland is the equivalent distance of riding end-to-end across Great Britain twenty times, or from Glasgow to Turkey and back three times, and nearly from London to Sydney and back again. My challenge was to ride as far as I could solo and sign off on at least three bucket list items. There are a lot of tar-sealed highways in Queensland, but where I wanted to go had a lot of gravel as well. Most of the good destinations in Australia require significant time on dirt roads.

Australia has long, solitary roads, deep sandy tracks, and dangerous bull dust and corrugated highways. My bike had to handle these conditions along with relentless heat and cold climates. It had several other criteria including it had to be LAMS approved, dual-sport, capable of carrying a full adventure rider's luggage, and finally, it had to be reliable. I also wanted a comfortable bike with a good reputation. Queensland can be quite hot during the summer, so a water-cooled bike might be advantageous.

Three bikes met my criterion, these included the Kawasaki KLR650, the Suzuki DR650, and the Royal Enfield Himalayan.

However, as I'm six foot two, I found the lower seat height on the Himalayan uncomfortable and its load-carrying capacity more suited to a lighter person, I still believe the Himalayan is an awesome adventure bike.

In the end, I chose the Kawasaki KLR 650. The seat height on the KLR felt right and it came standard with a windscreen, fairing, a water-cooled engine, and a twenty-one-litre fuel tank—additions I would need to add to the DR650.

I negotiate pannier racks, engine protection bars, bark buster handlebar protection, and an aluminium bash plate. I also got discounts on adventure riding gear. The total price for this adventure package was $13500.00. I would end up spending another $4000.00 before my 20,000-kilometre odyssey was complete.

Now, all I needed was to get my license and some camping gear, an understanding of what food I would need and how I would pack it all. My camping gear today is significantly different from when I started this adventure.

My goal is to ride around Australia, but to do it justice I would need at least four months, and I couldn't take that time off work or away from my kids who were just about to leave school and would need some help with this transition.

As I started to collect the items I needed, I became more and more confident. The more confident I became, the more outwardly I looked at the world, and the more opportunities I found sitting in front of me. I started to visualise my life on the road.

I'm a great believer in the power of the universe to guide you in achieving your goals, which is another way of saying there are infinite possibilities. You just have to tell it what you want and then do something—anything but sitting still and waiting. Vision without action is just a dream, no matter how long and often you dream it. Having a vision is the most critical part of the process because it enables you to select a course of action when infinite possibilities present themselves.

Friends of mine who have suffered from depression have told me how it saps their energy away and makes getting out of bed difficult. While the causes are not well known, there can be no doubt that a combination of genetic disposition and how they think over their lifetime has contributed to this illness. This is not a criticism; we can all reach this point. It's not an individual thing; my experience of watching life go by while sitting in an office is an example of the hopelessness that can take us down. If you keep thinking and feeling negative thoughts, then that's what the universe will provide in return.

Thinking you can do something will manifest itself in doing it; it might take some time, but it will happen. Along this pathway, you slowly build the skills and resources you need, which help motivate you to go further. At least, that's what happened to me. Like the little engine trying to get to the top of the hill, "I think I can, I think I can."

In my situation, I didn't have the financial resources to buy a motorcycle when I first put this plan in place, but an opportunity arose to do some contract work outside of my nine-to-five job, so I took it and worked nights and weekends. Eventually, I saved enough to buy my motorcycle. I now had a clear pathway to achieving my goal and a way to step out and just be me for a while. There was an excitement pervading my thoughts as I got closer and closer to starting my adventure.

I have found over the years that I was surrounding myself with trinkets, and other things that didn't add value to my life. These things were just patches created by society to mask the matrix in which I was living. I found myself going through life collecting more and more of these trinkets, tying me to the consumer lifestyle. To the point where I was feeling like a battery hen.

I found that the more I desired, the more the universe would provide, but there's always a cost that must be paid. That cost is the time we give to our employers, which saps our lives of meaning. In my case, it was sitting at a desk, tapping keys, shuffling paper, and watching birds fly freely in the sky. To what end do we trade our lives? Retirement, a lap around Australia, and then an aged care home?

What happens when those patches we have yearned for start to split and fall off? We have invested so much in them being the meaning of our lives that our lives become meaningless. This can happen for various reasons, such as a change in relationship dynamics or even a small bald patch that hints at declining virility.

I'm still not sure what caused me to look differently at the world, but I had just completed some meaningless task for the third time. "Fuck it," I thought, "time for a change."

So now I have my license and a sparkling new motorcycle. But I had no idea what a full month's adventure would require, or for that matter, where I would go. It's not until you start thinking about riding a motorcycle around Australia that you start to appreciate not only its size but its cultural diversity and history.

To get used to my new motorcycle, I took a couple of solo trips around my local area. I joined the North Queensland Adventure Riders group and went out on a few of their rides. After one of these trips, I started thinking I had better give my riding companion a name. In many cases, the name is feminine, but I was inspired by nature, so I thought a good Aussie name was a reasonable choice, so after much deliberation, I called him Emu.

Male emus have a very responsible role in emu society. They bring up the kids (as much as they can, since men bringing up kids is always a risky thing), and even look after other little emus that may have lost their families. The mothers take off on girls' nights and never return. My motorcycle was like an Emu; its job was to look after me, so that's what I called him. There were many times during this trip that I talked to Emu, we made a deal: he wouldn't crash, and I would clean his chain, replace his oil, and generally ensure regular maintenance. So far, we have both kept our promises.

I also started to think about our trip. How big is Queensland? I have driven across it several times; it's big, I mean massive. It's the second biggest state in Australia, next to Western Australia. It's 1,727,000 square kilometres, which might not mean much other than it's fucking big. Then you realise it is seven times bigger than the United Kingdom, five times bigger than Japan, and could fit two and a half states of Texas, USA. If you ever meet a real Texan don't tell him, size matters to Texans.

Fast forward six months and seven days, and I'm sitting on a cliff edge in central Queensland, my feet dangling over the abyss. My mind starts to wander, it's peaceful. I have everything I need to survive carefully packed on Emu, who is concealed as a bush with a camouflage cover over him. There's a sense of freedom, I guess. I can go where I want and do what I want. This is what it means to be a solo biker, to be free. There are endless possibilities, just waiting for me to turn right or left, or if I don't feel like making a decision, I go straight ahead. I start to think that life makes more sense sitting on this cliff edge than it does sitting in an office. I feel an awakening happening, am I on the verge of discovering the secret of life?

There's a great scene in the movie *City Slickers* where Billy Crystal's character talks with the cowboy Curley. Curley asks, "Do you know the secret of life?" Crystal says, "No." Curley responds by raising his finger and smiling, then says, "There's just one thing." And like all the people watching the movie, I've always wondered exactly what that one thing was. Maybe by the end of this adventure, I'll have found out.

Chapter 3
Twisting the Throttle

Every great adventure has to have a beginning, and this one is no different. The time has come to start Emu and head into the Queensland outback. It's a cool winter's morning, which differs from winter as it's known in other parts of the country; the tropics have their own weather descriptions. It's usually either hot and wet or hot and dry. I look up the road; the clouds hang low like a wispy blanket over Mount Stuart, and the navigation towers for the Townsville army base are almost entirely obscured by clouds. Just above the clouds, peering out like a lone sentinel, is the red light on the navigation tower.

It's been a slow start this morning. I have double-checked my bike and gear, ensuring all the straps are tight. It's unusual for me—I'm usually less obsessive about such things—but Emu has been packed for the past two weeks. It feels oddly surreal to put on my helmet, knowing this marks the start of a much-anticipated adventure, next I put on my glasses and then my gloves. This routine will become so automatic by the end of this journey that I'll hardly think about it. I have a mental block about taking my keys out of my pocket before putting on my gloves, so I take off my gloves and get the bike key, this too is a habit I find hard to change and one that dogs me for the entire trip.

I have a knot in my stomach and feel uncertain. I feel a strong force trying to pull me back into the house. Yet, I have been planning this trip for almost a lifetime. I wonder why I have these feelings. Something deep inside tells me I can't do it, that I'll crash, and the bike will be irreparably damaged. I recognise this as the inner voice trying to protect me, I'm fooling myself, that I'm not good enough.

Just as I start to feel that dreaded anxiety, a rhythmic tapping starts to pervade my thoughts, eventually it fills my consciousness, slowly getting louder and clearer: "Sitting in the morning sun, I'll be sitting when the evening comes, watching the ships roll in, then I watch them roll away again, yeah. I'm sitting on the dock of the bay, watching the tide roll away..." I start to feel the enticing excitement of endless possibilities, just like those days at Fisherman's Wharf on the Gold Coast. I can feel it beginning to grow like kindling struggling to ignite, more smoke than heat. Before long, a couple of flames appear. It's that spark I've come to count on throughout this trip, I don't understand how it can change my life. All I have to do is listen for now.

I turn the key, push the start button, and Emu fires up. The rev counter fluctuates as I twist the throttle, the choke's on and the engine's running rich. "Ready, Emu?" I say out loud, and I'm sure I hear him squawk, "Let's go." Rolling down the dew-covered grass of the front lawn and onto the road, I'm careful not to touch the front brake—it wouldn't be a good omen to have the front wheel slip out from under me at the start of my journey, not to mention the embarrassment. Letting out the clutch lever and twisting the throttle as I hit the road, I can feel the low-down torque that differentiates the older-style single cylinder from the more modern twins. Emu, fully loaded with gear, pulls away effortlessly. We've moved from indecisive children to adventurers.

I've just realised that I don't have a real plan, all this time planning and I'm not sure where I'm going. That's a strange feeling. I know I'm going out west—"To the outback and beyond." There are some other bucket list items I want to tick off, one of which is to rewrite the history of the poor old swaggie in the Waltzing Matilda legend. Another is to find or buy a boulder opal from Opalton.

Once I've done that, I think I'll head to the Gold Coast to catch up with some old mates, via Carnarvon Gorge, where I'll stay for a few days on a cattle property. From there, I'll start my trip up the coast of Queensland, photographing as many beaches as I can for my blog post, "The best beaches in Queensland." I want to catch up with some mates in Bundaberg.

So I guess I do have a plan after all: "Head west," then "south, at some point," visit some beaches, catch up with some mates, and drink lots of red wine. How much more detail do you need for a month on the road?

But it's more than just motorcycle touring; it's a rite of passage—an opportunity to do something I've wanted to do for a very long time. Thirty days on the road, just me and my bike, like two mates out on their first adventure together, not knowing what they will find. My panniers are packed and bulging, and my solar panel is stretched tightly over my top bag. I have packed to counter any eventuality, from total societal collapse and the much-anticipated zombie apocalypse to dinner with the Queen.

It's not until I look back at my home in the mirrors that I wonder what's at the heart of this desire to ride solo through the outback. I start to wonder what this journey will reveal to me about myself. There comes a time in the life of men when you are looking for more than your nine-to-five lifestyle. Women like to call it a mid-life crisis, I know that's too simple, but for the sake of marital bliss, let's just agree. How many times do we do that, when really what we want to do is say, "I'm not arguing with you, I'm just telling you why you're wrong"? How long would the silent treatment be after that outburst?

As I hit the first roundabout, my mind turns to riding. I catch myself wobbling slightly as I quickly adjust to the extra weight and its distribution on the bike. I've heard people say that getting on a motorcycle and riding away is a difficult thing to do, and I guess I understand what they mean. But once you're past that first corner and focused on the road ahead, that indecision and doubt are left behind. I have faith that I will be okay out in the world by myself. Now it's just me, Emu, and the road. Oh yeah, and all those crazy fuckers in cars that drive them like guided missiles and the suicidal kangaroos bouncing around in the outback. Still, it's time to trust in karma and know there are endless possibilities, now that I've put action to one of my dreams. It's no longer just a dream or a bucket list item, it's an experience.

The art of motorcycle touring is something that people who don't ride bikes can't understand. Adventure riding takes it to another level. Riding requires complete concentration; on the tar, it's okay occasionally to let your mind drift, but not too far, and certainly not on a dirt road. Full concentration on what's happening around you leaves very little time for negative thoughts.

When I was discussing this trip with a mate of mine and talking about getting lost in the outback, he gave me some good advice. He said, "Gazza, mate, if you get lost in the outback, find yourself a kangaroo and follow it. You'll be on the road in no time." If you're. not Australian, that probably doesn't mean much to you, but Kangaroos have a habit of finding a road to cross just as a car, truck or motorbike is coming along. They then hop out in front of said car, truck or motorbike, with obvious consequences.

I start accelerating to highway speed as I come up onto the access lane. To my right are the Townsville army barracks. There's a cold wind blowing on my face and an increasing noise of the wind pervading through my helmet. The cold makes me shiver slightly; I reach across my jacket to make sure it's tightened up to my neck. I'm merging now onto the highway and I gun the engine. It's a slow, methodical thumping sound until Emu gets up to cruising speed.

Even though the road is familiar, I feel a little anxious—or is it the cold air burning my lips? I have driven this road hundreds of times but only ridden it once before, on a small day trip to Ravenswood. Today is different; I'm feeling slightly exposed. I have a heavily loaded bike and there are big ore trucks from the port that I have to overtake, lest I get stuck behind them on the way up the Great Dividing Range.

The Great Dividing Range stretches from the Southern Alps of Victoria's high country (not high by New Zealand standards) to the tip of Cape York. It divides the fertile east coast from the dry Australian outback. More and more, it's also becoming a cultural divide between conservative farming communities and left wing progressives in the city. The invisible line between is like a self-imposed fortification for the very woke, middle-class Australians who very rarely venture across it. The ride from Townsville to Charters Towers is all highway; it has some spectacular scenery as I race by pastoral properties, small ghost towns, and eucalypt forests. The road is well maintained, and I'm comfortably sitting at 110 kph.

There's plenty of time to think and plan as you ride down the seemingly endless highways in Australia, this is often called helmet time. My mind starts to wander to all sorts of places. But I'm soon brought back to the here and now by a large bridge, crossing the Burdekin River. My first stop is a free camping site just out of Charters Towers, called "Macrossen Park." The park is on the eastern side of the Burdekin River, but you can easily miss it if your concentration is on the expanse of the bridge straight in front of you that spans the Burdekin River and not on the small sign notifying you of the park.

Turn left at the dirt road, then ride about two kilometres towards the river. It has a barbeque facility, a toilet block, and areas for you to camp hidden amongst the bushes. I make a note to come back at a later date and maybe stay a night.

The first hour and a half of my adventure has been enjoyable and while I would like to stay here longer, I also want to make some distance from Townsville before retiring for the night. The top of the Great Dividing Range is much cooler than the humid fertile land of the east coast and the dry windswept plains of the outback. For this brief moment, I'm enjoying the cool winter weather while I can. I know the further west I go, the hotter and drier it will get.

Parked next to one of the many barbeque areas in the park, I take advantage of the shade to make a coffee. Emu is fully loaded and looks like a real adventure bike, stacked full of equipment, food, and camping supplies. On his seat is a BeadRider cover; the beads are meant to keep your backside cool and massage it while you ride. It only half works; my arse is starting to feel sore, the stock KLR650 seat is notorious for being uncomfortable. The experienced guys in the riding group say you have to just ride through this and your butt will toughen the more you ride. I hope this is true.

I get to the main road and turn left; below me is the majestic Burdekin River. I marveled at the engineering feat it would have taken to build this bridge. It's about 30 metres above the river bed and can be covered by water during a heavy wet season. It's worth stopping on the western side of the bridge to marvel at the height markers, where the river flowed over the bridge and up the hill.

In 1946, the river flooded to its highest point of 21.8 metres, barely surpassing its previous 1870 level of 21.7 metres. Early signs of global warming? You decide. It's hard to imagine the size of this river during a flood. I remember crossing it one wet season and working out that approximately 1.56 gigalitres were passing under the bridge every minute.

My mind is brought back to the task at hand. I feel a sharp bump as I hit the eastern access to the bridge. Emu is carrying a lot of weight for this trip, and I have a lot of weight over the front wheels from having my tools and spare tubes in bags over the engine crash bars. I'm not sure this is a good idea, but he seems to be responding well, and I feel comfortable as I ride over Macrossan Bridge. Picking the right gear for this type of adventure is quite difficult; the decision relies on understanding where you're going and what you intend to do. And as I had no idea of either, I just packed for every eventuality. But I couldn't help questioning myself and my selection of gear.

It's not long before I'm on the outskirts of Charters Towers. As I ride around, I'm met by remnants of its mining history, gold mining to be precise. It wasn't long after the mass influx of miners looking to make their fortune at Ravenswood, one of Queensland's biggest gold rushes in Australia, that gold was discovered in this area. The gold might have stayed in the ground a little longer had it not been for a lightning storm and a spooked horse. After the storm, an Aboriginal boy named Jupiter was sent to find one of the horses that had broken loose in the middle of the night. He found the horse in a small creek; as he gathered the horse, he noticed something shining in the water.

It was 1871 when Hugh Mossman, George Clarke, Fraser, and Jupiter prospected approximately sixty kilograms (1660 ounces, or three million dollars' worth at today's rate) of gold from the region. Mossman went into Ravenswood to report the claim. The mining warden at the time was William Ewbank Skelton Melbourne Charters. The claim became known as "Charters Tors" and was later renamed "Charters Towers."

The allure of gold is everywhere in Charters Towers. Opportunity at every dirt mound. The town grew rapidly as miners flocked to the new gold field. Many of them were frustrated by the lack of easily obtainable alluvial gold in Ravenswood, and yet, gold is no longer mined in Charters Towers but is still mined in Ravenswood today.

Other prospectors continued even further north, looking for the headwaters of the Burdekin River in the hope of finding the gold seam.

I stopped at a small mining display on the Charters Towers bypass road to have lunch. Pulling out my camp stove, I boiled some water for coffee, peeled back the foil on my tuna and rice mix, and rationed out a couple of muesli bars.

This was to be my go-to lunch for most of my outback motorcycle tour, at least until I could find a bakery. It was simple and provided the energy I needed to continue for the next couple of hours. After lunch, I took the opportunity to explore Charters Towers.

The town is a living history and is a great example of many different architectural styles, the most dominant of which is Art Deco. As more miners arrived, the easily accessible alluvial gold started to disappear. In a unique show of socialism, groups of miners got together to purchase more complicated extractive mining equipment.

A cooperative was formed to keep track of individual investments and to manage the purchase of equipment. An exchange was set up to manage each miner's stock. In 1890, the Charters Towers Stock Exchange was opened. The miners could trade these exchange notes like currency. The uniqueness of this business model at the time was such that the everyday man or woman could be owners of capital, not something that was possible in Mother England at the time. As the practice continued, miners were issued with stock notes. The mining exchange predated the first official stock exchange in Melbourne, Australia, by two years. It's interesting that what we see today as the cornerstone of capitalism, the stock exchange, was established by a group of socialist miners in the outback gold town of Charters Towers, Australia.

As the town and infrastructure grew, there was significant investment flowing into the town from England through the newly developed stock exchange. Many of the shares were bought up by foreign investment capital from the mother country, making the miners wage earners again rather than capital investors.

With miners losing their independence again, Charters Towers became a hotbed for new socialist/communist ideas and the rights of the individual working person over the more traditional rights of capital or the feudal system of the landed gentry. The miners were hard-working and resented people telling them what to do. It had only been 16 years since the Eureka Stockade, and the reforms and ill will that led from that massacre were still in the minds of Queensland miners. This is the reason you see a lot of the Eureka Stockade flags throughout Queensland even today.

Learning their lesson from the Eureka Stockade, the miners resisted armed rebellion and formed the first mining union in Queensland. Members of this mining union would later help the shearers in the great shearers' strike of the 1890s. The main crushing and processing plant was situated on the only hill overlooking the town, not far away from the main diggings. The ride up Towers Hill is worth doing, if you're in this part of the world; it's the site of the old pyrite works, and there are examples of mining history on display. The majority of this activity occurred around the hill. Historical signs and markers describing the formation of Charters Towers are displayed on the walking trail that meanders up the hill. The hill itself played a role in the Second World War as a communication station, part of the Northern Australian network that conveyed messages from the front line. It was also a repository for ammunition supplies. Tunnels and mine shafts dot the hill, with many bunker entrances visible as you ride up the road.

Motorcycle touring and adventure riding are growing in Australia, and in Queensland, for anyone looking for their first adventure, I would recommend Charters Towers as a good place to start. The town is a well-preserved city of late classical and early Art Deco design, which gives it an air of the 1920s. There are many places to explore around the town and some free creek-side camping. But as I still wanted to make some distance before nightfall I wanted to continue west.

I have done a lot of "wild" and "stealth" camping over the years, but I'd never been camping and motorcycle touring. This was my first official night camping on my motorcycle tour of Queensland, my destination was about halfway between Charters Towers and Hughenden at a place called the Campaspe River Rest Area. It was getting late in the afternoon and I needed to keep riding for another hour and a half.

The sun was starting to go down, the golden light was darting through the scrub and tall eucalypts, and flashing uncomfortably, while the western sun wasn't low enough to blind me, it was getting onto that time of day when kangaroos like to cross the road looking for food, which wasn't available on the other and probably the safer side of the road.

Pulling into a large, grassed area just off the highway, I took a moment to circle the grounds. There was a toilet block, a large mango tree, and plenty of room to set up camp. On the western side adjacent to the road and tucked into the bush were four caravans parked neatly and in single file next to each other. Each had a small fire glowing next to the van and a little terrier-type dog of some sort yapping on their leashes. The first of many grey nomads I would encounter on this journey. They are an interesting breed, secretive, suspicious, and quick to hide back into their shells at the first sign of danger. As if to highlight this point, as I rode around the park a second time, they had vacated their fires and yapping dogs and were nowhere to be seen, perhaps filling up their glasses with Chardonnay.

There was plenty of space in this off-the-road camping area. I circled the grounds one more time before getting off my bike and going for a short walk. It felt good to take my helmet off and casually stroll around, hunting for the ideal spot. I wanted to be as far away from the road as possible to avoid the engine braking noise from large trucks, which seemed to be a common practice near rest areas, lest anyone was trying to rest. This mostly occurred after midnight, making me wonder why braking seemed easier during the day when air brakes were rarely used. Still, I guess even truck drivers need a hobby. I was looking for a place to camp where late-arriving vehicles wouldn't accidentally run over me. The only safe spots seemed to be under the eucalypts or gum trees. Unfortunately, eucalypts are known to drop giant three-tonne branches on unsuspecting campers.

So, staying well away from them was a necessity. I eventually settled on a small grassy site tucked into a space near the mango tree and well away from any track where a vehicle might drive through in the middle of the night or, for that matter, anywhere near the smelly toilet block.

I set up my camp for the first time on a motorcycle trip. It included setting up my bunk, inflatable mattress, pillow, sleeping bag, and a small collapsible chair. I also brought with me a Biolite Stove as a backup. The Biolite is a fire stove that has a battery and fan. The heat from the stove powers a little battery charger, which can power the fan and has enough charge left over to power any of your electronic accessories. I had been looking forward to using it since I bought it, and now was the perfect time. I scratched around to find enough twigs and small branches and before long, I was cooking dinner and charging my phone. After dinner, I packed most of my gear back onto Emu, put a camouflage cover over him to keep the dew off, and settled into my two-man dome tent, silently drifting off to sleep.

Chapter 4
Life on the Road

The pressure wave lifted me off my cot and shook me awake; the light and noise shattered the early morning peace. It was like the arrival of an alien spaceship, or at least what I think one might sound like. I heard people moving and car doors slamming. The rest area seemed like a hive of activity. Looking at my watch, it was three in the morning—what the fuck was going on? Between the vehicles coming in at all hours of the night, the trucks with their engine brakes, and the train with its bright light and earth-shattering horn, I had managed to get about four hours of sleep.

Opening my tent to peer outside, it was still dark and cold. I could see the faint outline of people moving around, the occasional beam of light from a torch. It wasn't a good time to hit the road, so I tried to go back to sleep. I made a note to find quieter campsites in the future. My carefully chosen campsite away from the main road and truck noises just happened to be right next to the carefully hidden train lines. I can't imagine why they thought they needed to use their horns at this exact spot at this exact time. I glance over towards the grey nomads; not a light on at all. How did they sleep through the train horn and all that traffic noise? Maybe there are advantages to hearing loss as you get older.

I went back to bed but only lay there staring up at the green tinge of the tent fly, even the soothing engine braking of a large Kenworth couldn't lull me back to sleep; it had left me. I might as well get up and make a coffee. There were some sticks and small branches left over from last night; instead of getting my gas stove out, I lit the Biolite stove and watched the flames jump and dash around until the water was boiling in my billy.

The Biolite stove was one of those luxury items that ordinarily you wouldn't take on a bike. But there was peace of mind knowing you weren't reliant on gas all the time. It's also really good if open fires are banned; the Biolite is considered a stove, not an open fire.

It was a stunning winter's morning, cool and crisp. I sat and watched the sky change from its inky purple to bright orange and then gold as I zipped my down jacket together to prevent heat loss. I was looking forward to getting back on the road; it was perfect riding weather. After breakfast of muesli and coffee, I packed my gear, found space for all the necessary items, repacked a couple of times, and then managed to get on the road. Two hours after finishing my last coffee, it was still only seven-thirty in the morning.

Riding along the Great Dividing Range early on a crisp, clear winter morning brings serenity that I'm sure only bikers understand. There was very little traffic on the road, and the kangaroos had long since left to find a leafy tree to sit under. The dark grey road is muted in the morning light; it feels cold as I wind up the small escarpment, then I come out onto a flat area and slow down for the small sleepy town. There is no sign the residents are awake yet. If only I had an air horn, why not share the love?

I went past the sleepy town of Pentland and then climbed up a winding road until I reached the lookout for White Mountain National Park. I had considered wild camping here; it looked reasonable on the map, but having found a peaceful, quiet campsite on the Pentland River, I pulled up there instead. Looking at the small table and shelter perched on a rocky escarpment, I think I made the right decision. The view over the White Mountains seemed so out of place with the dry red dirt and eucalypt scrub of the country I had been riding through so far. The hills disappeared into the horizon as far as the eye could see; it was spectacular, and I hadn't expected to find such wilderness in this part of Australia.

The first stop after White Mountain National Park is Hughenden. The road is straight and edged by eucalypts and traditional Australian bush flora. As I ride down the range, I start to feel a change in temperature. Up to this point, there was still some humidity in the air, but as I descend the western side of the Great Dividing Range, the air becomes drier and the vegetation turns more brown than green.

The further I go, the drier it gets—I think this is called the Outback. Have you ever wondered why it's called the Outback? It's a mystery that I hope to solve on this trip. There's another term used in Australia, "the bush." I start to wonder if the bush comes first and then the near desert landscape beyond the bush is known as the outback. That would make sense, "outback past the bush." Now if I only knew what constitutes the bush.

On the left, up in the distant hills, is a wind farm with about one hundred giant white monolithic structures, their giant rotating blades and ominous shadows casting strange shapes across the dusty, dry plains. I'm not sure if it was because I was getting tired or if it was my imagination playing tricks on me, but I imagined the slow movement of a giant alien army across the flat, dry plains of the outback, with their slow-turning mechanical arms reminiscent of the film *War of the Worlds*. Maybe these were the aliens I heard this morning.

Hughenden was built on the banks of the Flinders River, which is key to its development. The river flows from Western Queensland to the sea and was first discovered by Europeans when Lieutenant Stokes of the survey ship *Beagle* located an estuary and river mouth in 1841. However, it wasn't until Europeans ventured into what was to become northwest Queensland in 1861 that the geographical survey showed the area was the headwaters of the Flinders River. A year later, William Landsborough's party camped on the site of the current Hughenden in yet another attempt to find Burke and Wills.

After reporting the expansive open grassland, there was a race to claim the most fertile parts of the land. Of course, nobody bothered to ask whether the land was already owned by an indigenous race of people who resided there at the time. Earnest Henry assembled eight hundred head of cattle and raced from Bowen to the region to claim grazing rights. The town was named after the English manor house owned by his uncle, where Earnest Henry had spent his youth, Hughenden Manor.

Today the town is a modern support centre for the pastoral community in northwest Queensland and one of the larger towns in the Flinders Shire.

I'm starting to feel a little hungry, so I look around for a park. There's not much in town, so I ride down to the causeway over the river. On the other side is a lush, green grassed area with barbecues and shaded tables. I ride Emu between the marker posts and find a shady spot under a tree. It's starting to get hot, so I strip off my heavy riding jacket and lay on the well-maintained grass. I could fall asleep now; it's the second day of my adventure, and I'm starting to wonder if I'll ever get fit enough to finish my journey. My butt's still sore.

It's a little early for lunch, but I know the road ahead doesn't have any rest areas that can compare to this riverside park, so I take out my stove and my prepackaged tuna and rice combo. I boil my billy and relax under the shade of one of the barbeque tables, keeping a wary eye on the local birds who seem intent on stealing my lunch or any other interesting-looking object.

This is my first experience with the outback bird mafia, and I do my best to prevent any unwarranted attack by making sure all my bags are closed and any tasty-looking morsel is hidden from view. After a short break, I go down to the river to take some photos of the dry riverbed of the mighty Flinders River. It's difficult to picture what it would look like when the river flows.

It's not long before my desire to continue overrules my need to stay where I am and rest. I put on my helmet, glasses, and gloves and start Emu. I ease Emu into a small turn and head back to the main road, then west to Richmond following the sign. The road to Richmond is built on a black soil plateau. The crosswinds try to drive me off the road while the constant bumps add to my fatigue. It's a dry, long, flat, energy-sapping torment. The excitement I felt when hitting the road had long since dissipated with every crosswind or road train pressure wave that hits me.

It's so devoid of trees and hills that you can see the horizon as you look across hundreds of thousands of acres of grassland.

The landscape is dry and almost barren, apart from the parched grasses and prickly pear weeds that seem to thrive in this harshest of lands.

Emu was cruising at 110 kph at just under five thousand revs. The temperature gauge was normal, and he didn't feel in any way stressed. I, on the other hand, was starting to feel tired; my butt was sore, and my ears were ringing from the continuous wind noise. About halfway to Richmond, I found a rest area where I could take a break. There was a peaceful solitude about being in the middle of a great expanse of grassland. I stretched out on the picnic table and had a couple of microsleeps—a practice I would repeat often on this trip.

I became acutely aware of the stillness and peace of the place. You can drift into thoughts of what this land must have been like a hundred million years ago when dinosaurs roamed the shoreline of what was a giant inland sea.

It was time to keep going, so I hit the road again, and within 30 minutes I was entering Richmond. The most famous resident of this town is the giant *Kronosaurus* statue at the "Kronosaurus Korner" fossil centre. The statue is a life-sized replica based on a fossil found in this area. The real creature would have been swimming around in the sea over 250 million years ago. These aquatic animals would have been the top predators of this area; I couldn't imagine a more fearsome beast. Richmond is at the northern end of the Northwest Queensland dinosaur trail, which extends to Lark's Quarry west of Winton.

Richmond was founded on the site of the pastoral lease Richmond Downs, which was in turn named after the Richmond River area of New South Wales. Both Walker and Landsborough had camped in the exact area of the current Richmond township.

Its development grew as a result of gold discovered in 1880 at Woolgar, north of Richmond. Over the years, it became a stop for stagecoaches en route to the goldfields in the north and Mount Isa to the west. It was surveyed as a town in 1882. I fuelled up at the modern roadhouse, bought hot chips and a coffee, stuffed the chips into my jacket, and headed over to the man-made lagoon, a main feature of the town. As I sat under the shade of a small pavilion, lying on the table to stretch my back, I became aware of a family of ducks staring at me. A word of warning if eating hot chips: the ducks are masters at getting food from weary travellers. One duck will walk out front, pretending to be friendly with a slight limp, while others come in from behind unseen. This is a well-practiced routine; I had chips taken from me in what I would consider a well-rehearsed pincer movement. It seems that motorcyclists make an easier target, so if you stop at the lagoon and you have food, beware of the bandit ducks.

In the middle of the lagoon was a small island, and just in front of me was an aluminium floating pad. It's a favourite place for people to come and practice their golf swing. The island is called "Dead Man's Island." It's the exact spot where the first European person to die in the area was buried. His final resting place was preserved when they built the lake, marking his burial site as an island in the middle of the pond, a thoughtful sign of respect. Then they built a platform and allowed people to use his final resting place as a target for golf balls. I hope he liked golf. If he didn't, it would be a kind of eternal water torture for the poor fellow.

Navigating your way out of Richmond isn't difficult; there are only two ways to go, and a big sign tells you where you're going in case you get lost or aren't sure which direction you came from.

The road to Julia Creek was more of the same, approximately 125 kilometres of undulating tar and harsh, unforgiving dry grassland. I was getting tired at this stage and was looking for a place to pull over and camp for the night. There's not much in the way of potential wild camping areas that are not directly exposed to the main highway. I did pull over a few times to stretch my legs, but other than a single rest area, there was no other opportunity for respite; I just kept riding.

Arriving at Julia Creek, I was more than ready to stop for the night and find a place where I could have a shower. I've been told by one of the grey nomads I met at a rest area just out of Richmond that the Julia Creek Caravan Park had outside baths that were heated by waters from the great Artesian basin. I thought that one lone biker with a small tent might just squeeze into the campground. Unfortunately, there was no space for non-powered single tenters like me, only powered sites for vans (apparently). So not only were my hopes dashed for having a nice outside bath with artesian waters, but a place to stay in town was also out of the question.

I was starting to feel travellers like me were unwelcome in these areas as many of the facilities and resources were focusing on the grey nomads and their mobile retirement villages. The lovely lady at the desk suggested I check out the showgrounds because they had space for camping.

The showgrounds were just south of the town centre, offering free power, hot showers, and clean toilets. The wind was strong, which made pitching my tent an interesting experience. The wind that had dogged me all day was still blowing hard as the sun was starting to go down. I had just finished struggling to set up my tent when the wind dropped and the most magnificent sunset lit up the sky. The galahs, who had been madly chattering away, stopped to look up at the darkening sky and this amazing outback light show. The large bright dot that was the sun slowly sank over the horizon, and as it did, the bright gold sky around it changed from gold to orange and then to dark blue, with all the colours of the rainbow in between.

There's nothing like an outback sunset, and just then, the evening star appeared, creating that perfect tranquillity in the campground with an uninterrupted view of the universe. There must have been at least a billion little lights covering the sky.

It was the perfect moment for a glass or two of red wine. I decided to make a quick trip into town; it was refreshing and enjoyable not to be wearing all my body armour and boots for this small trip, which made the ride immensely enjoyable.

At the bottle shop, I was presented with an eighty-dollar bottle of wine. I knew alcohol was expensive in these remote towns, but this was ridiculous. I was wearing my black Kevlar jeans, black gloves, and black down jacket, with my helmet menacingly threaded over my right arm. I was a biker, not the affluent owner of a mobile retirement home. At one metre eighty-eight centimetres tall and weighing one hundred fifteen kilograms, I must have looked a little intimidating. The young man at the bar sheepishly produced a bottle of house wine for eight bucks, which was much more in line with my palate and wallet.

I rode back to the campground with a feeling of exhilaration. The spark that had been lit when I pressed the starter only two days ago was starting to catch fire, and I now knew the next month on the road was going to be adventurous. As I watched the sun go down, I thought of the next stage of my trip and what awaited me in the western Queensland outback. Tomorrow, I would start working towards my first bucket list item. I sat back in my chair and felt content to be at last at the beginning of a great adventure.

Chapter 5
Hunting Ghosts

Hunting down a ghost is not what you think of when you're reading about motorcycle travel. Today is day three of my journey and I'm sitting on my small travel chair with my feet perched on my collapsible travel table as I take in the expanse of the Julia Creek Showgrounds. I'm thinking about the road ahead where I finally hope to encounter the elusive ghost of the dead swaggie from the song "Waltzing Matilda."

It's early morning, and the grounds are bathed in the golden light of another magnificent outback sunrise. The galahs are busy scratching out seeds and chattering incessantly.

I've just had a hot shower at the showground facilities and I'm excited about today's adventure. My itinerary is to ride to the Combo Waterhole and find the ghost of the murdered swaggie, where the song was thought to have been written. For years, I have sought out the ghost of the poor old swaggie in the song. According to the song, the ghost may be heard as you pass by that billabong. I have also discovered a backstory that I have wanted to write for over 20 years. It just happens to be the number one item on my bucket list.

I'm anticipating a short ride down an outback dirt road to Kynuna, then about 12 kilometres on the Matilda Highway to a muddy dam called the Combo Waterhole. I'm undecided as to where I will go from there but had contemplated stealth camping at the waterhole in anticipation of the ghost that may be heard. If I go north, I will reach Cloncurry; south will take me to Winton.

One of the pleasures of motorcycle camping in the outback is that it allows you to sit and watch the sunrise. Sunrises and sunsets in the outback are spectacular, with golden and red light giving way to clear blue skies. As soon as the first rays of light penetrate the black inky sky, the galahs and cockatiels wake up and start their incessant chatter. This morning there was no wind, the sky was crystal clear and the birdlife was prolific and noisy.

The day doesn't start until the first cup of coffee. To make my morning coffee even more special, I brought with me a coffee pod pump. You simply put the coffee pod in the pump, add a small amount of hot water, and pump the little plunger until all the water has passed through the pod. Then, fill your cup with boiling water, milk, and sugar, and presto—you have barista coffee in the outback. I'm starting to think I have brought too much gear and I start to contemplate sending some of it back home. I have a bad case of cognitive dissonance about the coffee pod machine.

Every little bit of bulk adds to the volume and therefore wind resistance, and extra weight reduces the power-to-weight ratio as well as wearing Emu's tyres faster. I'm already feeling I have overloaded my bike. I will have to think about what I'm carrying the further I get into this journey.

After a breakfast of muesli, coffee, and a couple of crackers with cheese, I pack up and go through the normal routine. Most of my fellow travellers have left already; as I ride out, the showgrounds are almost empty. I have to refuel before hitting the road to Kynuna.

Julia Creek is an ideal stop on a ride around Queensland; it has a pub, servo, bakery, and a showground. What else could you ask for? The town is like an oasis, a hive of activity with trucks, cars, and caravans going in all directions. I'm keen to get on the road, so I quickly refuel Emu and ride out of town. I'm eagerly anticipating my first patch of dirt, but become devastated when I find the road to Kynuna has been tar-sealed all the way. As I ride out of town, the land seems almost barren, the dry straw-coloured grass quickly fades as the dry dark brown dirt hints at a season without water. It seems almost dead; the earth is cracked, and the bones of cattle are everywhere. From out of the sun, a squadron of cockatiels dive towards me, flying just above my head like an honour guard.

Their presence almost blocks out the sun with grey and yellow wings and deep orange dots on their cheeks. I can vaguely hear their chirping as they whirl and dart around me; it's a magnificent moment. They fly with me for about two hundred metres before one yells what I think means "Look, water!" and they wheel in formation and head out to a nearby waterhole.

It's a beautiful scene, the crisp fresh feeling of cool wind, the deep blue sky, and the well-worn cattle tracks on the side of the road. Now and then, another flock of birds flies by. The image of my honour guard will stay with me; it was such a random yet perfect moment that it lifted my spirits. I was to experience many of this events throughout my journey, I call them "Wow" factors; they would often change my mind set and make me feel alive. It's the sheer beauty of nature that takes my breath away.

I happen to look in my mirror; close behind me is a small 10-ton cattle truck. I pull to the left, slow down, and signal for him to pass, but instead of overtaking, he slows behind me. I stop, then he stops, so I take off again, and he toots his horn at me.

As I turned around, I could see the driver getting out of his truck. He was an older gentleman in his 60s, one of those genuine country characters. "G'day mate," he said, "I think you've lost something from the side of your bike," pointing at the right pannier. I responded with "G'day." Looking down, I could see one of my dry bags was missing; it was the one with my tent in it.

"Oh, fuck," I say.

He laughed. "It's about twenty kilometres back. I couldn't stop in time, but I'm sure someone would've picked it up by now. Try the twenty-four-hour roadhouse in town; people often stop there," he said. I thanked him and turned around. "Shit, another forty kilometres to my journey." But my camping plans will change without a tent; I'm relying on it for stealth and cheap camping.

As luck would have it, I was just taking off my helmet to go inside the 24-hour Caltex station when a young man walked up to me. "Have you lost a green dry bag?" he asked. I nodded. "I left it at the police station," he said.

Thanking him for his kindness, I jumped on Emu and headed to the police station. True to his word, my dry bag and tent were at the front of the station—an amazing show of country spirit and generosity. Mate, if you read this book, thanks for your help. Many bikers travel around the world without tents, but I think a tent is the foundation of freedom on a bike. It's your home away from home, a bit of security you can rely on if you're ever caught without a place to stay.

When I thought I had lost my tent, a small panic button went off. With a tent, I could stop anywhere; without it, I had to find a town before nightfall.

Back on the road to Kynuna with the heat starting to pick up as the sun rose higher, it became more evident how dry the ground was. There were small spirals of dust swirling up from miniature tornadoes called dust devils. Now and then, I rode past the bones of dead cattle and occasionally these carcasses were near waterholes, the skull of a cow that couldn't survive long enough to outlast the dry season. And yet, with all this dust and dryness, the creeks had water in them and the dams seemed full. I crossed causeways with water lapping at the sides, while up on the flats, the ground was fractured. There were cattle on both sides of the road in good condition, despite the lack of grass.

It wasn't long before I got to the end of this rural connection road and joined up with the aptly named Matilda Highway. To the left, the road to the Combo Waterhole, and the road further south to Winton. To the right, the small town of Kynuna and the road north to Cloncurry. I turned right and arrived at Kynuna five minutes later. Parking Emu at the curb I headed straight for the pub as you do. Kynuna's not a big town; actually, it's only a pub and a petrol station. But the pub had chairs outside, so it looked like a more relaxing place to sit and take in the passing traffic. There were a couple of tourists sitting on the veranda when I pulled up and a couple of others trying to fix a small car problem. I thought this is not a place you want to have a problem with your car.

The Blue Heeler Hotel is one of those quintessential Australian pubs that seem to be in a time warp. I have read several motorcycle stories over the years, the first one was in the now obsolete *Pix People Magazine* (which I only bought for the stories) some forty years ago. Then in my early 20s, I enjoyed the articles and, of course, the pictures of the topless bar maids and the party atmosphere, thinking to myself this looks like the place to be.

At the time, I had no idea where it was, and it wasn't until I lived in Mount Isa I was able to put this area into perspective. Three "must-do" items sprang up from that realisation: Larks Quarry and its famous dinosaur footprints, boulder opal from Opalton, and finding that bloody ghost of the dead swaggie.

Sitting on the veranda overlooking the Matilda Highway, I watched tourists and road trains pass on their way to more exotic destinations. Stripping off my jacket, I sat under the shade of the veranda and enjoyed a ginger beer, with the slight breeze from the dusty plains providing some relief from the relentless heat, dust, and flies.

It is slowly dawning on me that while it is important to plan, one should try and stay as flexible as possible when on the road. I pulled out my map, laid it on the table, and surveyed it for my destination. There it was, the infamous "Combo Waterhole". During my previous visit to the area in 2001, I had spent four hours digging my four-wheel drive out of the black soil mud in the car park.

At the time, it had occurred to me that there was something not quite right about the song. For a start, after four hours of digging my car out of the mud by hand, there was no sign of a ghost, not even a laughing, sniggering one enjoying the spectacle. Secondly, most people who had visited the waterhole reported it to be a small shallow pond, hardly big enough for a wise old swaggie to drown in. I had always wanted to come back and write the real story behind the "Waltzing Matilda" myth.

The Combo Waterhole is a fantastic piece of engineering for its time. While the view of a single billabong tends to pervade most conversations, the combo in the title belies the multiple water catchments around the area.

The trip out to the birthplace of one of Australia's most loved songs, "Waltzing Matilda," is an easy ride today, but in the time when "Banjo" Patterson wrote the song it was a rest spot for the Cobb and Co stagecoach. Getting there today is a tar-sealed road with a toilet block and car park at the end of the road. When I came here in 2001, it was a dirt four-wheel drive track, and a muddy one at that. I parked Emu near a shaded table, out of the sun and walked around the small self-guided walk. As I walked around the small interpretive walk that has been built for tourists, I learnt about the engineering behind the site and the Chinese labourers who built it. The billabong, or waterhole with its historical foundation and the myth of the old swaggie, should be a rite of passage for all Australians.

But what happened on that fateful day when the poor old swaggie committed suicide is a mystery that puts the credibility of the song into doubt.

The historical foundation of the song has fascinated me since childhood. I've always wondered why the "swaggie" just gave up, no resistance, no protest, jumped into the billabong, and drowned. As a kid looking at each billabong I passed on our family vacations in Victoria, I wondered, "Is that the billabong?", "If we're quiet, will we hear the ghost?" Alas, it was not to be. About twenty years ago, my wife and I moved to Mount Isa for work and I finally found the site.

I'm back here now to have a good look around and to try and understand what might have happened on that fateful day and, if possible, solve this mystery. I'm going to retrace the footsteps of that poor old swaggie and try and get the real story of what happened that fateful day over 106 years ago.

Chapter 6
The True Story of Waltzing Matilda

Waltzing Matilda is one of those great Australian icons, like the Opera House and Barry Humphrey. It seems larger than life, but it's a tragic story set at the time of Australia's European birth. Waltzing Matilda is a part of Australia's identity and a defining story of Australia's colonial history. It somewhat defines the Australian culture. If you're not familiar with the term "swaggie," it refers to an itinerant worker who used to carry all his possessions in a bit of canvas that he rolled out as his bedding wherever he camped for the night.

This is a tragic story of an old swaggie trying to survive in a hard, unforgiving environment. It is lamented in the song, "Waltzing Matilda" that every Australian knows. It starts with this swaggie camping out in the middle of nowhere, when "Down came the Squatter riding his thoroughbred, down came the policemen one, two, three..."

That's probably the only true statement in the whole song; the rest is myth-making. The story of that ill-fated exchange between a law-abiding swaggie camped out near a stagnant muddy swamp, in the middle of a stinking hot desert landscape and the aristocratic landholder with his police lap dogs.

I'm sitting under the shade of an iron roof at a concrete table, the small modern toilet block is at the end of a tar-sealed parking area just behind me. I look out to the Combo Waterhole in front of me and try to transport myself back in time. What would this place have been like in 1893 when the song was written? Even today, the flies are annoyingly abundant, there's not a breath of wind, and it's hot. If the waterhole had water, there would have been birds, bees, and bugs all swarming around. The sides of the waterhole are cracked mud and the water an orange muddy soup. Maybe there are the bones of old dead sheep, the stunted frame of coolabah trees, and spinifex shrubs. It would have been quite apart from the chirping birds and the laughter from "Banjo" and his crush at the time, Christina Macpherson, the sister of the owner of Dagwood Station, who it is reported were having a picnic.

It's difficult to completely create a fictitious character and a situation from scratch, so there must have been an existing situation. Banjo and Christina might have been discussing some recent events, and Banjo started putting a poem together. I'm a little sceptical about the whole swaggie killing himself in a muddy pond, so bear with me as I deconstruct the story, knowing what I know about swaggies.

"Whose that jumbuck that you put in your tucker bag?"... Now, here's a problem for the popular myth of a downtrodden swaggie and the belief that he stole a sheep and just gave up. The swaggie was a shearer, which we know from Banjo Paterson's later writings. The swaggie would have been quite militant and possibly even part of the striking shearers. The great shearers' strike of the

1890s was in full revolt. It is more likely when confronted by three police officers the swaggie said, "What jumbuck, this is old kangaroo?"

Swaggies might be a little down and out but they're not fucking stupid. The swaggie probably also said, "Now fuck off and leave me alone, (copper scum)." Now the cops could have grabbed the tucker bag and had a look, but as far as we know they didn't, and it would be almost impossible to prove anything unless there were the obvious signs of the old sheep lying around like fleece and all the blood, but this wasn't mentioned.

The swaggie is a battler and the quintessential underdog, which is, to some extent, how Australians see themselves. This is the story of the underdog, the little guy standing up against the injustice of the ruling elite. Was the swaggie in the story making a stand against injustice or just trying to get some food for his family? Either way, it didn't work out well for the poor old bastard... did it?

I understand why people find this song appealing; it has been played all over the world, wherever Aussies have fought against injustice or during times of great sorrow. It was played as the first ANZACs left Sydney Harbour for Gallipoli. It represents a certain freedom of choice and a degree of self-determination. Whatever the motivation for the song, it's a window into the birth of this great nation and the struggles of the working class. It has a similar plot to the demise of the infamous bushranger "Ned Kelly," "You'll never take me alive, copper scum," but they did and then hanged him in Melbourne Gaol.

Did the swaggie know there would be no justice and decided that death was better than being sent to gaol?

If we dig a little deeper, there are several theories as to the identity of the poor swaggie. One of the more popular beliefs is that he was one of the shearers who organised a violent revolt at MacPherson's "Dagwood Station," where the Combo Waterhole resides. This has a lot of merit as it was the family property of Christina MacPherson, who wrote the music to "Waltzing Matilda," and possibly the topic of discussion at her picnic with Banjo.

It is reported this shearer was the ringleader of the shearers who burnt down the woolshed, which killed 143 sheep. He then ran off into the night. His name was Samuel Hoffmeister, a French-speaking shearer from Batavia.

It is well documented that Bob MacPherson (the squatter) and three police officers went after Hoffmeister, but according to court records, turned back due to light rain. This made the shearer's footsteps difficult to track. Now, if you believe that, you might also believe in honest politicians and fairies at the bottom of the garden.

I don't pretend to be an Aboriginal tracker, but if it rains, the footprints become as clear as mud, maybe… just saying. It turns out that Hoffmeister got to within eight miles of a shearers' camp at Kynuna before sitting down and shooting himself in the back of the head.

In the sanitized version of the event lamented in the song "Waltzing Matilda," the swaggie does something completely out of character. He gets up, thinks "fuck this," and dives into the billabong and drowns, "You'll never take me alive," says he. To add insult to injury, he manages to drown in six inches or less of water.

The troopers didn't even bother to jump in and help. It's a muddy swamp for fuck's sake, I think there is something seriously wrong with how this was reported.

Now, I'm not saying there's corruption at play or that Banjo decided that the truth would have made the swaggie a martyr, which may have inflamed an already tense situation. It wouldn't be too much of a stretch to think some of the facts may have been covered up, like the bullet hole in the back of the head… just saying. Maybe Hoffmeister was double-jointed.

Can you imagine the true verse, "And the Squatter drew his rifle and shot the swaggie in the head, 'I'll never take you alive,' said he"? It doesn't convey the same kind of message. What the song does tell us about the history of Australia and the people who lived in this harsh land is that they were hard-working class battlers. They weren't just battling the elements of an unforgiving land. They were battling an unjust legal system and a feudal social order where the landed gentry had more rights than the working man. Maybe the song says that, in a roundabout way. In 1894, Australia wasn't even a nation as we define nations today; it was part of the British colonies, and the British were in the midst of the greatest industrial revolution of all time. They (meaning the industrial class) needed as much wool, gold, silver, and copper as they could lay their hands on. The shearers' strike was an inconvenience, and an armed rebellion so soon after the war of independence in the American colonies was something they couldn't afford.

When I learnt "God Save the Queen" at primary school in Melbourne in the 1960s, I had already been singing "Waltzing Matilda" for a couple of years in the back of the family car on those much-loved country holidays. It is almost inconceivable that this song, which today still inspires a nation, was written about an incident at the Combo Waterhole in the middle of the Western Queensland Outback. While the myth surrounding the death of the poor swaggie at the Combo Waterhole carries on into history, the myth-making didn't stop there. It is reported that after a few drinks, the shearers' strike ended and everybody was mates again. It must be true because it was reported by none other than the great "Banjo Paterson" himself. This story is recounted on a plaque on a wall inside the Kynuna Hotel. Proudly displayed is what we could call today "False NEWS."

It says that "through this window in 1894, Banjo witnessed the squatter McPherson (Dagworth Station) pass Champagne to those very shearers who had burnt their woodshed." "And in so doing the shearers' strike ended." But let's not let the facts get in the way of a good story.

We must appreciate one very important point in what has been recorded here. In 1894, in a small pub in the very heart of the Australian Outback, when it takes at least three weeks to get from the port to the pub, where did the champagne come from? Not only that but what was the demand for Champagne that made it viable to transport it to this small remote pub that serves mostly shearers and cattle barrons?

Whatever the story and however you want to interpret the events of that fateful night at the Combo Waterhole in September 1894, there is no doubt that a legend was born.

This act of defiance and the consequences that played out that day, defined so much of who Australians are as a nation. It cemented the role of the Aussie Battler and made a hero of the underdog.

When I was a kid in the back of Dad's station wagon on those long Christmas holidays, I remember thinking that every waterhole we passed was the one from the song, and I would listen for the sound of the ghost. In the song, "the ghost can be heard as you pass by the billabong." Sitting on the barbeque table, with the sound of birds and insects I closed my eyes and listened for the ghost, but as usual, heard nothing. If you're out here, listen—maybe you'll hear him. If you do, ask him what happened on that night and let me know.

One really important useless fact about flies: they are suicidal. They try and steal food from your mouth as you eat it. Sitting under the shade of a corrugated iron roof, I ate my lunch of tuna and the occasional fly. It was time to move on, so I packed my gear and rode back to Kynuna for more fuel.

I was in two minds on my way back to Kynuna: Do I continue to battle the elements for an extended period of hot, dry, and dusty riding, or should I start making my way south to a cooler climate?

As I fuelled up at the Kynuna petrol station, I watched two massive road trains pass by, carrying mining equipment. Even at the bowser of the station, I could feel the hot pressure wave given off by the massive trucks. The dry red dirt whipped into a swirling mass of angry dust that blocked out the mid-afternoon sky before settling on everything around it, including me.

Dealing with trucks is a given when you're on a motorcycle; it shouldn't influence your decision. It was decision time, and I made up my mind to turn south and head directly down the 170 kilometres of the aptly named Matilda Highway to Winton.

The sun was well overhead, and I could feel the heat radiating off the tar-sealed road. Emu was purring at a comfortable speed of 110 kph. The wind noise was starting to annoy me and my seat was becoming unbearable again; it was good to be on the final part of my journey today and I was glad I didn't increase the length of my ride today.

I was thinking about how disappointed I was that once again I hadn't heard the ghost when, without warning, I was hit by a strong, powerful supernatural force from my left side. It's hard to explain, but it was like a constant wind pressure wave. I thought maybe it was the ghost of that old swaggie. It was so strong it pushed me over the centre line and into what would have been oncoming traffic. It wasn't your typical wind gust; this was like a giant unseen hand constantly pushing me, all of it happening at 110 kph.

The only thing I could do to counter the force was to lean into the wind and drive the bike back into the left lane. Emu and I were leaning at about a fifteen-degree angle into the wind. No sooner had I done that than the wind changed direction from the right, and I found myself out of control, being driven off the road. The white line that differentiated the tar-sealed road from a fifty-millimetre drop-off and corrugated dirt siding was only a hairline away as I fought to keep Emu on the tar.

What is this unseen force of nature, I thought? There was no dust, no movement on the side of the road to indicate wind direction, then just as quickly as had appeared, it was gone, and I flew into the centre of the road.

The road was quiet again; the spinifex whipped past, followed by endless kilometres of barbed wire fencing on both sides of the road. It was hot and dry; nothing was happening, the only sound was wind in my helmet and the thumping of Emu's engine. Once the initial adrenaline faded, a lot of things went through my mind. What was this strange force in the middle of nowhere that seemed hell-bent on killing me?

Suddenly, it happened again, but this time with almost twice the force. I was leaning to the right, trying to hold onto my handlebars, and keep Emu within the white road marker lines when I spotted a chip packet about five metres in front of me going in the opposite direction.

It occurred to me that I was in the middle of what, in Australia, is called a "Willy Willy" or "Dust Devil." I have seen these things as big as a small tornado. At this point, I understood, and as the chip packet got closer, I prepared for the sudden wind change. On cue, the wind changed direction, I managed to keep the bike in the middle of the road as the chip packet sailed over my head. I was to encounter one more of these strange, natural phenomena.

As I got closer to Winton, the flat, dry grassland was broken up by small sandstone escarpments. These relieved the boredom of nonstop grassland and spiky spinifex. As the sun started hiding behind the hills and dropping ever lower towards the horizon, I could feel the heat start to ease. I rode past camping opportunities, and for some reason, I wanted to get to town and find a caravan park. There are several places I could camp tonight which are about fifty kilometres north of Winton. A group of caravans had found some flat land and created a semi-circle. I slowed momentarily but decided to continue, even though I was tempted to just pull up and find a suitable flat place to camp.

I have faced this dilemma a couple of times on this trip: when I got to Richmond, why not just look for a campsite? Always the question: should I stop and camp or just continue? It would have been an ideal place to stop. I might have met some new people and who knows what adventure that might have created. Time is an interesting phenomenon; when you make a decision, it changes your life forever. Do I go right or left? If I go right, I know where I will get to, but if I go left on an unplanned route, who knows where I'll end up and what endless possibilities will I encounter?

This, I think, is the true essence of adventure: when you're riding down one path, you stop and camp, something changes in your mind, and instead of continuing on, you stop for the night. Before you know it, the path you were on before is not the path you are on now. I guess this is the essence of karma; your decisions determine your path in life. I wonder if it is the fear of the unknown path that prevents people from venturing down it.

After a long, hot, and dry 170-kilometre ride from Kynuna, I arrive in Winton. The light is starting to fade as the sun hits the horizon; the sun seems to get larger as it sinks, creating a giant ball of white surrounded by a golden aura. It's not long now until it will start to get dark. I can already see the inky blue sky starting to form in the east. I found a non-powered campsite at the Winton Caravan Park and set up my tent and sleeping kit for the night. I cover Emu and then go for a walk into town to find something to eat.

Chapter 7
Land of Dinosaurs

The long hot ride to Winton yesterday took it out of me. I'm not riding fit yet, and the seat and wind noise make for uncomfortable riding. It had taken longer than I thought, especially with the head and crosswinds that buffeted me along the road. The land around Winton, and in this part of the country generally, looks sparse, but it's teeming with life. From snakes and kangaroos to bird life of all types. Strangely, this is the home of sheep herding and cattle production, but for the life of me, I can't understand why. I can't see a sheep anywhere, but I have seen lots of emus and kangaroos running and bouncing around.

The big red kangaroos, which can be over two metres tall and weigh more than ninety kilograms, start to come onto the road at about four o'clock in the afternoon, so travelling on a motorbike at this time becomes hazardous.

Winton is a town of contrasts, from its historical support town for the sheep and cattle industry to becoming a modern-day tourism and opal mining centre. There are so many aspects of Australian culture that emanate from Winton, yet it is one of those places that seem to be "too far" out of the way for your average tourist.

The town is also the centre of the dinosaur trail that started in Hughenden. There are dinosaur foot bins, a dinosaur museum, and out of town, a giant dinosaur park called the Age of Dinosaurs, which is one of the most interesting and spectacular dinosaur displays I have ever seen. Apart from the fossils found around the area, Winton is also the gateway to Lark's Quarry, which is one of the only places on earth to have recorded a dinosaur stampede. It is believed that a flock of small herbivore dinosaurs was being chased by a big carnivore. The footprints can be seen clearly in the fossilised mud of what was a small inland waterway.

There are many interesting places to explore in and around Winton, but the one day I have allocated to explore the town just isn't long enough. I intend to take it easy today and just walk around the town, hoping I can find out more about the history of the town and what the road conditions are like on the road to Opalton. Getting to Opalton and finding an opal is the second item on my bucket list for this trip.

The distance between cattle stations, towns, and any local services in this part of the world is immense. It's no wonder that when the airplane came along, graziers and sheep farmers were the first to take advantage of this new form of travel. Airplanes were soon seen as a way to bridge the tyranny of distance in the Australian outback. It's strange how circumstances conspire. There are differences of opinion as to how QANTAS came into being. One story is that a Cloncurry man, Fergus McMaster, became stuck crossing the local river when another man by the name of Hamish Griffin came to his assistance, and discussions about airplanes came up. The pair hatched a plan to create an air service.

They got together and created some investment funding, but needed more money and also someone who knew about flying, so they took the idea to a group of cattle and sheep farmers in Winton. The first official meeting of QANTAS, Australia's national airline, was held right here in Winton. When looking at the old nondescript building where the first meeting was held, it's hard to believe that it was here one of the biggest airlines in the world had its beginnings.

The Winton Club was a place for the well-to-do of the area to meet and socialise, like a country club of sorts. There was no shortage of investment funds for innovative ideas to help people and goods move around the country. Air transport must have seemed like magic at the time. If you're on a tour of Australia or planning one, don't just ride through Winton. Take your time and explore; there's more under the surface than you might expect at first sight. Stop for dinner at the famous Winton Club, sip a cocktail at the Art Deco North Gregory Hotel, or catch up with some opal miners at the local Winton Hotel.

If you spend the time to look around, you will see another side to this remote outback town. I walked around the town and couldn't help noticing how practical the houses were. They reminded me of Mount Isa, mostly fibreboard and corrugated iron. They were built to reflect the heat, not store it like some sort of brick and tile heat sink. Unlike modern houses in urban areas, the ones in Winton don't need air conditioning all year round despite the great summer heat.

There are reminders of the region's history everywhere, like the old ploughs built into Arno's Wall or the rusty old Ford trucks that sit like gnome ornaments in the front gardens. Winton is definitely a town with a lot of history and character, the town people seem to pride themselves in having the biggest, rustiest contraptions in their front yards.

The town is full of contrast, from the old rusting cars and Arno's wall to the stately and rather grandly named Royal Theatre.

I have felt for some time that I was slightly overloaded. I spent the morning sorting out those things I thought I wouldn't need. This included a second pair of shoes, a second jacket, a slingshot (don't ask), a camping pot, bits of clothing, and several books. All in all, it weighed twenty kilograms. I packed this into a dry bag I was carrying and sent it back home from the local post office. I still feel I'm overloaded, but I'm not sure what else I don't need.

While I was in town, I sought to find out more information about Opalton and the condition of the road out there. As I walked around Winton looking for opal shops, I couldn't miss the North Gregory Hotel, not only is it the biggest building in town, but it's also the most famous site in Central West Queensland. It is said to be the home of "Waltzing Matilda." It is also one of the best-preserved examples of Art Deco architecture in Queensland. The North Gregory Hotel is a sublime example of the wealth of the town in its heyday.

In a small room just off the dining hall is a piano, and above the piano is a sign that says, "It was here that 'Waltzing Matilda' was first sung." A copy of the actual song sheet and words accompany the song and the piano it was played on. But here's the rub—it wasn't.

According to records on the wall of the Kynuna Hotel, it was first played there to striking shearers. This particular version of the North Gregory Hotel is the fourth in a long line of burnt-out boarding house taverns. If the song was indeed played here, it was in version one of the hotel. The North Gregory was always a "posh" hotel; the country was living off the sheep's back and there was no better place for sheep than out here.

At one point, it was estimated that the local area contained 11,854 head of cattle, 99,515 head of sheep, and 5,652 horses. That was in 1891 when there were only 625 people in the area.

It's difficult to go past the "Waltzing Matilda" legend when you're in Winton. Imagery is everywhere, from the man-made billabong at the entrance to town, to the giant "Waltzing Matilda Museum" and accompanying statue of its favourite son, "Banjo Paterson." There's even a statue of the "swaggie" from the song. Unfortunately, he's on the opposite side of the road, tucked in behind a couple of trees.

Sitting down on the park bench next to the statue, with the town swimming pool at my back, I looked across the road to the opulent tourist centre, with its bookshop and city-style café, I felt out of place. The KLR650 wasn't your café racer; it was the workhorse of motorbikes. I thought of the "squatter mounted on his thoroughbred," which in today's terms would have been a rather expensive Ducati or a BMW. Wasn't this a cruel sort of irony?

As I pulled out my gas stove, water, billy, and coffee-making equipment and settled in to make my brew next to the swaggie statue, it occurred to me. What would I do if the cops arrived, pointed their guns at me, and told me I'd stolen my food? Would I give them the finger and jump into the swimming pool to drown myself? Probably not. No, I'd probably tell them to fuck off.

But Winton is more than Waltzing Matilda, in the back streets behind the North Greogory Hotel is a truely remarkable site. Stand aside, Great Wall of China, you have been outclassed by Arno's Wall. It is a uniquely Winton monument, built by Arno

Grotjahn, a German immigrant who came to Australia in the 1960s.

Arno's Wall is a uniquely original masterpiece and reflects the man himself who was recognised as quite a character in his own right. As a young man, he was a merchant sailor before joining the French Foreign Legion. In his thirties, he came to Australia with his wife and settled in Winton. He spent most of this time, when not opal mining, building his wall.

One of Arno's ancestors stood alongside Peter Lalor at the Eureka Stockade, which is why there is a giant Eureka Stockade flag painted on the wall. It's in honour of his ancestor and a sign of defiance. The wall itself is over seventy metres long and, according to Arno, is a monument to machines and a way for him to display his collection.

I walked around the town admiring the architecture then realised it was time for a beer and where better than the North Gregory Hotel Beer Garden. As I sat there looking out over Arno's masterpiece, I thought Arno must have known the "one thing." Maybe my future was in building a wall like Arno's. My mind drifted and I could hear the song in my thoughts, "The Dock of the Bay." I wonder where I could build a wall.

Maybe when I get home, I should consider building a wall like Arno. The thought quickly exited my mind almost as fast as it had arrived. I'm not sure how my wife would take it if I built a 70-metre wall with old bits of machinery around our house.

Chapter 8
Gunslingers and Opal Miners

The galahs had started their early morning chorus, long before the first cockerel had even stretched its wings, I wondered if there was a competition among them to be the first bird to sing out, so much so that they forgot to worry about if the sun is coming up at the time. But today, that competition suited me. I needed to be up early; this was going to be a long day. I would ride out to Opalton, then if all worked out ride back to Winton, fuel up, and head southeast to Longreach.

The path to Opalton is a dirt track. It's your typical outback cattle road that contains corrugated corners and deep red bull dust holes in a sparsely maintained near-desert landscape. If you survive the journey, you discover this little (one would be overstating it to call it a town) shanty community. It's a frontier community of miners and tourists. I couldn't pass up the opportunity to find or buy a boulder Opal. It had been the number two item on my bucket list for some time.

The journey to Opalton in Central Western Queensland started over 34 years ago in a rather expensive jewellery shop in Martin's Place, Sydney. At the age of 23, I had gone to Sydney on a holiday. As I walked through Martin's Place, my eye caught the flicker of a gold ring with an amazing multi-coloured stone in its centre.

Venturing into the store, I quizzed the very knowledgeable shopkeepers on everything I could think of about this magnificent stone. I discovered for the first time what an opal was.

In the middle of the deep brown stone with black and gold lines running through it was a deeply translucent and highly polished opal. The blackness of the stone highlighted the blue, green, and red opal, which changed colour and intensity as I looked at it from different angles.

The lady at the counter told me it was a boulder opal surrounded by iron stone, which as the name suggests is as hard as iron. When asked about its origin, she told me it was from Opalton in Central West Queensland. Was it just curiosity or had I instantly succumbed to opal fever? My obsession grew by the minute; the thought of getting my hands on my very own boulder opal was overwhelming. The next day, I procured a map, but to my dismay, Opalton was in the middle of nowhere—well the middle of the Queensland outback.

Over the years I had thought about its location, wondering if I would ever be able to get there. It was chalked up as a bucket list item. You know, one of those things that you want to do but didn't think you would ever get to do. Over the years, I had driven past Winton and each time lamented on a trip out there, but it just seemed too far away and too dangerous. Isn't it interesting how we talk ourselves out of doing things because they just seem too difficult? When, as I have learnt from this adventure, if you just do it, karma will take care of the rest. I guess the Nike phrase, "Just do it," applies to all sorts of adventures.

During this time of procrastination, I read a lot about opals and opal mining in Australia. There were mysterious disappearances and claims of murder, stories of gunfights over claim jumping at Lightning Ridge. People I talked to said how opal mining wasn't for the faint of heart.

It seemed there was a Wild West in Australia and it was Opalton and Lightning Ridge. I supposed that is why the price of opals was so high, you had to be pretty tough to work the claims.

Fast forward 34 years and today is the day, I'm going to make my way out to Opalton and get myself one of them boulder opals, or die trying. I'm not sure what I will find or if I will be able to ride there, I guess that's why they call it adventure riding.

Yesterday I visited many of the opal shops in town, and there are quite a few. The shopkeepers are more than happy to share their knowledge of opals and Opalton. Having topped up my opal knowledge and researched the track conditions to Opalton, I felt ready for the journey. One of the shopkeepers pointed me in the direction of the local pub, where rumour had it the opal miners hang out when in town. "If I wanted to know the current track condition, I would be best to ask one of them," she said.

I intended to make friends who would back me when the going got rough or who could at least handle a six-shooter. I tried to learn as much as I could about the little town with the big reputation, in particular where I could expect to be ambushed by bushrangers or claim jumpers.

The air is cool and the sky is clear, so this is an indication of a hot and sunny day ahead, a typical winter day in the outback. Droplets of dew drizzled down my tent fly and Emu's camouflage cover. The chill was enough for me to put on my down jacket as I fired up the camp stove. The day doesn't officially begin until the first cup of coffee. As the sun was just starting to change the dark blue sky to an inky purple, I could see the first rays of gold appearing over the road east to Longreach.

As I finished my second cup of coffee, the thought of riding 238 kilometres of lonely outback dirt track on a fully loaded adventure bike was a little bit intimidating. Although I was heartened by the reduction in weight after sending some non-essential items home yesterday.

I brushed my teeth in the sulphur-smelling water that comes directly from hundreds of metres underground in the great Artesian basin and which I'm told is millions of years old (Probably pee'd in by dinosaurs as well). I flick some more of the foul-smelling liquid over my face, pack the bike, and head through town to the dirt road out to Opalton.

The sun was now over the horizon, and it lit up the road sign like a spotlight highlighting that Opalton is 119 kilometres, Lark's Quarry 110 kilometres.

There's a beautiful crispness that engenders the sheer joy of riding at this time in the morning, especially when you're riding through a near-desert landscape of low-lying hills and sandstone flats. The sun is on my back and the morning air is crisp.

Unfortunately, it's also a time for kangaroos to wander around after their night activities, and hitting one of those would certainly bring an end to my motorcycle adventure of Outback Queensland. The kangaroos are big out this way so I wasn't excited about hitting the road early, at least until the sun had come up. I had to be fairly certain that any self-respecting kangaroo had hopped away from the road.

I wanted to investigate a free camping ground just out of Winton called Long Waterhole. Long Waterhole is just a big dam with excellent camping sites among coolabah and gidgee trees. It has steep sides that go down about eight metres to the water. There are several trees around it and some flat areas for parking; there was a lot of evidence of cattle having watered there, as the place was potholed with hoof prints, clearly at a time when the banks were softer. I wonder if this will perplex scientists millions of years in the future, "Look, evidence that ancient cows flocked like birds?"

There were approximately twenty large "off-road" caravans and expensive four-wheel drives at the waterhole. They were set up in a horseshoe configuration with the open part of the shoe facing the dam. A classic defensive pattern, I thought to myself, clearly there have been problems with bushrangers or even some of those giant kangaroos I had heard about, and this was how they fought them off.

I left the waterhole and decided to ride slowly to enjoy the morning light while I could. If the past four days had been anything to go by, I knew the temperature would soon increase as the dew was burnt off and the full force of the sun fell over the track.

Just out of Winton is the Bladenburg National Park; it's a dry, seemingly barren landscape, with clay pans, sunburnt Mitchell grassland, and gidgee trees. In places, you can easily see the worn-down sandstone plateaus, deep trenches, and the occasional sandstone monolithic statue like something from Stonehenge, which is typical of the channel country. When it does rain out this way, long flat clay pans like this form rivers that feed inland to the centre of Australia and pool in Lake Eyre.

It was a surprise to see several big red kangaroos out here; they are usually more solo travellers, and they can grow over two metres tall. I see two very large kangaroos standing on the track. I'm a little bit intimidated by them and as I ride closer, they seem in no hurry to leave the track. It's almost like they are border guards or standover men, I briefly think to myself, "I'm going to be fleeced of all my possessions by these two giant red kangaroos; how am I going to explain this to the insurance company or even show my face at the next adventure riders meet?"

As I get closer, they put their heads down and quietly shuffle off the road to munch on some interesting bit of grass that has taken their eye, or is this just part of their ambush plan? I look around but can't see any compatriots in the wings. My mind wandered back to the settlers with their wagons drawn around at the Long Waterhole and their defensive strategy, and then it all became very clear to me.

As I ride on further into the park, some gullies indicate river courses, and I head down one of the tracks that promises to open up into a watercourse. On the left side of the track is a small sign that says "Historic Shearers' Camp." I'm tempted to go down this road and have a look, but I am also conscious that I have 224 kilometres of dirt to ride today.

It seems I'm riding deeper and deeper into the National Park; while the environment is breathtaking, it's not getting me closer to my goal for the day, so I turn around and retrace my tyre tracks.

Had I not put this tight schedule on myself, I would have explored the region more, and I make a note to return sometime to do so. I find a couple of sandstone monoliths and use one to rest my camera on while I stand next to the other for a selfie.

Within no time, I arrive back at the Opalton Road and turn off to see a couple of the settlers and their mobile retirement homes depart back to Winton. I turn left and continue up the main road. Shortly after this, the road turns to dirt, and I begin the first dirt section of my adventure.

It feels good to be on the dirt; my senses have become more alert, not only for the kangaroos making their way home, but when riding on dirt you can't afford to let your mind wander, lest you come into a corner too hot or you hit a patch of bulldust, which in both cases can signal disaster.

The road in this early part of the journey is good, and I don't encounter much in the way of potholes or bulldust. I'm not an expert in riding dirt roads, so I stick to about 70 kilometres per hour, a speed I feel comfortable doing on my bike with its current load and my ability or lack thereof. The road to Opalton is spectacular, going from long dirt straights to winding through small low-lying sandstone bluffs. It's an adventure rider's dream road with lots of sweeping corners, jump-ups, and corrugations.

I estimate that it will take approximately two hours to travel the 112 kilometres to Opalton. I'm conscious I have 50-50 tyres and excess luggage, all of which conspire to slow me down and make riding more difficult.

Riding over one small jump, I come across the worst road I've encountered in my short riding career. It's on the top of the ridge, with long straight sections of corrugations that continue around each corner. On the sides of the track and in the worn areas are deep sections of red bulldust. It seems never-ending; each section lasts for about two kilometres and then the track opens out leading me into a false sense of security before the next two or three kilometres of terrifying torture.

I do know that keeping a good line, not crossing over, and bringing my weight back as far as I can seems to help. I also notice if I drop down a gear and rev the bike slightly higher in the corners, I have more control as the bike exits, allowing me to select a better line. So, I do this at each section, and I find I start to ride more confidently. Once out of the ridge country, I pull over and take a short break; I've been riding now for one and a half hours.

It takes two hours and twenty minutes to ride the one hundred and nineteen kilometres from Winton to Opalton. When I get to the town sign, I'm disappointed not to see a note telling me to leave my guns at the saloon. Does this mean I was foolish riding all this way out without guns? The township would be a short distance away, so I rode down the flat gravel road expecting at any minute to find the main street.

To call Opalton a town is a bit misleading; it is a collection of makeshift shanty dwellings with an arrangement of caravans and the odd fridge placed strategically as a sign. I continued riding past a shanty shed and caravan, which was the Opalton general store.

After about five minutes, I came across a few more caravans and a small sign saying Opalton Caravan Park, which appears to have several old caravans and a couple of old containers perched on stands. One small building that looks slightly more substantial than the others has a small veranda and a vending machine.

An old guy was sitting on a weather-worn plastic barbecue chair. The little veranda area had about five small tables and an assortment of mismatched furniture. A rather flashy sign just in front of the veranda of the old building indicated it was a visitor centre. A handwritten scrawl on an old blackboard out front read "Back Four PM." The author of this message was probably sorting out a feud between two rival opal gangs.

Emu and I pulled up to the tin fence at the side of the hut; I reversed back to ensure Emu was out of the way should any stray bullets come his way. It felt like I should have tied him to the hitching post. Following my now well-used ritual, I took off my glasses, then my helmet, followed by my riding gloves. As I turned around, I saw the old bloke move slightly. This is it, I thought, no sooner had I arrived than I was going to be gunned down.

"G'day mate, where have you come from?" he asked, with a youthful grin that belied his seventy-five years of age. Jim was the most welcoming guy I had met in ages, and we talked about all sorts of things, but mostly about Mount Isa. Jim was in town to visit his long-time mate and fellow ex-Mount Isa miner.

As I had worked for three years in Mount Isa at the beginning of the millennium, I knew a lot of the town and people in it. Unlike other towns where you have to be born there to be a local, Mount Isa is the type of town that has so many different cultures that if you have been in town for a year and you had a job, you were a local.

So here we were, two local Mount Isa boys sharing a cold glass of water. That was until an Opalton local appeared by the name of Dave who drove up in his dusty Navara Ute. Dave had been in Opalton for five weeks working a claim and was now considered an expert local miner. Dave was probably 30 years younger than Jim and had come to Opalton after his divorce and the loss of his fishing fleet in Normanton, which consisted of two rusty old boats.

I learnt a lot talking to these two awesome men. When asked why I came all the way out here, I relayed the story about Martin's Place jewellery shop and my bucket list item. At which point Jim pointed to the tap and said that if I wanted to find some opal without having to blow up one of the hills, try your luck over by the tap. Apparently, miners use the water in the tap (which is supplied by a local dam) to help chip away at rock that is likely to have opal through it and if I'm lucky, I could pick up a bit of opal for myself.

The trick is to water the rock fragments and turn them over, looking for shiny bits that might be opal. I washed the dust from my face and began shifting rocks looking for that elusive opal. I must say it was exciting work; the prospect of finding that million-dollar stone was addictive. I found a piece and quickly tucked it into one of my inner pockets. "It's mine, my precious," I said to no one in particular.

Bob turned up and took his sign down; he was the custodian of the information centre and ran a small opal sales business for the local miners. I mentioned that I wanted to buy a piece of boulder opal, so he opened the shop and showed me some amazing bits of stone. I eventually settled on a piece and a price. Tick off one item on my bucket list. It feels good to be ticking off such a long-standing bucket list item.

Unfortunately, my time in Opalton was limited as I had decided to ride to Longreach, which is three and a half hours away. It would have been great to camp for a night and learn more about the town. Bob offered to take me out to a working mine. Opalton is a place I would like to visit again. I said goodbye to my new friends; Jim came up to me and gave me four different rocks, each laced with opal. I shook their hands and thanked them; what an amazing group of people.

The ride back didn't seem to take as long or seem so difficult. I had started to perfect my bulldust riding technique and I knew what was coming up. It became a way of riding sand or bulldust:

heavy rear brake once I see it, brake in a straight line, wash off some speed and set the back shock, set my line, release the brake, and accelerate.

Something is enlightening about being alone with your thoughts for an extended period. My mind wandered to my father who had passed recently at the age of ninety-two. He wasn't a great father; he was never there for us kids and exhibited a very narcissistic attitude towards us and our mother.

But I felt sad for him. He loved gemstones, the Australian Outback, and "Waltzing Matilda" and was still riding his R1150 RS at the age of 74. He would have loved this trip and had he been a different person could have spent 30 days just riding and camping with one of his sons. It would have been one of those rides that build memories. I made a mental note to encourage my son and daughter to one day take a ride with me before I become too old to ride these sorts of tracks. It's moments and adventures like today that forge lasting memories, even once someone has passed. I arrived back in Winton at about three in the afternoon. It's a two-hour ride to Longreach, so I refuelled Emu and headed south.

First night camping - Campaspe River Rest Area

Australia's first stock exchange – Charters Towers

Kronosaurus Korner – Fossil display – Richmond

Duck mafia, hot chip bandit – Richmond

Emu outside the Blue Heeler Hotel – Kynuna

Murder of the old swaggie, Combo Water Hole - Kynuna

Waltzing Matilda first performed – North Gregory Hotel, Winton

Art Deco interior – North Gregory Hotel, Winton

Arno's Wall, Winton

The author and Emu on the way to Opalton - Bladenburg National Park, Winton

My bolder opal purchased from opal miners - Opalton

Showdown the infamous visitor centre - Opalton

Opalton city centre - Opalton

Friendly raptor, Age of Dinosaurs - Winton

Chapter 9
My Religious Experience

The road to Longreach was like the road I had ridden into Winton; it was long and flat, the wind was hot, and periodically tumbling tuffs of weeds would blow across the road ahead of me, reminding me of those old black and white Western movies with John Wayne and Clint Eastwood. The dust would float momentarily in the air and form small clouds of yellow mist.

My bike seat was becoming unbearable; I had been in the saddle too long and I needed a break. I had intended to stop and camp at an isolated site out of the way of passing traffic, but I couldn't find one. The grassland spread out before me to the horizon, there were no trees, shrubs, or bushes of any kind to hide me from the road and I felt too exposed to the trucks whizzing by at all hours of the night. There were only five metres of land on each side of the road before the barbed wire fence, which was put in place to keep cattle and sheep from becoming roadkill.

It was late afternoon and even though it was still winter, it was hot. There is a hot dryness to this sparse and unforgiving land; in summer, it could reach well into the 50 degrees Celsius range, but in winter it could drop to below freezing. I thought about the swagmen travelling this land looking for work; they would have trudged this path for days without any shade or water.

Luckily for me, times have changed. At about 70 kilometres out of Longreach, I came across a small rest area. It wasn't a place I could camp but it gave respite from the road. It was a small flat section of dirt with a small raised toilet block, a shaded concrete table, and a rubbish bin. There was enough room to park a couple of cars, then about a metre of dead dry grass and the barbed wire fence. The only way I could camp here would be to have a hammock, which in a cruel twist of fate I had sent home from Winton.

I had got into a habit of cooling off and relaxing by stretching out over the concrete tables of rest areas and closing my eyes. I knew I had to carry on, but for now, a short micro-sleep was in order. My mind again drifted back in time as I listened to the wind blowing the grass and the shuffle of the gravel from the small willy-willies twisting in the heat of the day. In the 1800s, this would have been a well-trodden path for swaggies and shearers. They would have known the best places to camp for the night from fellow travellers; who knows, this might have been one of those places.

I could hear a distant rumble; was I hearing thunder? As my consciousness returned to the present, I could make out the telltale rumble of a big Harley Davidson. Before long, a big black gleaming Road Glider pulled into the parking area. It was closely followed by a sweet-purring Yamaha FJR1300 Sports Tourer. I lifted my head as the two bikes parked next to each other and the riders removed their helmets.

Bikers come in all shapes and sizes; the Harley was ridden by a short, stocky grandmotherly woman wearing a leather jacket, black riding jeans, and a shiny black full-faced helmet. The other rider was wearing a mesh adventure jacket, blue riding jeans, and a more racing-style helmet. I estimated both riders were in their 60's. It appears they were a semi-retired couple testing out their new bikes on a small road trip. I couldn't help feeling there was more to this couple and their mismatched selection of bikes. They were planning on riding the same path as I was, so hopefully, I would catch up with them for a longer conversation down the road.

We talked, as bikers do, about where we've come from and where we're going, but before long it was time to go. As I put my jacket and boots back on, they disappeared with a rumble into the heat haze towards Longreach. It was time for me to finish this day and find somewhere to camp for the night.

The micro-sleep and interesting conversation pepped me up, and it wasn't long before the signs indicating I was approaching Longreach came into view. Longreach is a major support town for the agricultural communities in the area; lately, it has become a tourist hub for all sorts of adventurous people.

Longreach was originally the tribal lands of the Iningai people. It was an explorer William Landsbourough who was the first European to see this area in 1862. Following the discovery of the wide-open grasslands, the Bowen Downs cattle station was surveyed and settled. The town was gazetted in 1887, a post office opened in 1891, and the rail line was put through in 1892.

After the First World War, the government was looking for ways to encourage air travel. Sir Hudson Fysh and Paul McGinness, two World War One pilots, were tasked with surveying possible aircraft landing strips across western Queensland and the Northern Territory. The long days of travelling through the harsh countryside in a Model T Ford gave them plenty of time to hatch a plan to establish an air service connecting remote communities. When in Winton, they met Fergus McMaster and formed Queensland and Northern Territory Air Service (QANTAS) in November 1920.

Longreach was the perfect place for such an endeavour and in 1920 it was chosen as a site for a new airport. QANTAS was officially formed at the Winton Club in 1920 before its headquarters was moved to Longreach in line with the development of the new airport.

I'm relieved to get into town as the sun is starting to set behind me. In the distance, I can see the red tail wing of a giant Boeing 747 SP with its red tail and white flying kangaroo logo; it's a fantastic reminder of the importance Longreach plays in the history of Australia.

A sign indicating a caravan park appears and I waste no time booking in and setting up my tent. As it happened, this was right next to a church group with guitars playing the joyful lyrics of "Kumbaya, my lord, Kumbaya." I think to myself, "How lucky am I?"

It was one of the better camping areas I had come across on this trip so far; it had a small park area away from the non-powered campground, just far enough that the 26th round of Kumbaya drifted away in the wind. As I sat brewing my coffee, I contacted my family to let them know where I was. It's strange, you want to tell them about all your experiences, but just seem to know it won't mean the same to them as it does to you.

The night became silent as my neighbours sang themselves to sleep. I finally fell asleep myself, only to be woken up as the sun was rising by those pesky rainbow lorikeets, who I'm sure were singing, "Kumbaya, my lord, Kumbaya," or some variation of it. Don't they know what bloody time it is? And can't they sing a different song?

I've always thought the lorikeet to be a typical Aussie juvenile larrikin; they love to eat the berries from the rubber trees, which they always eat too much of, get drunk, and fly into buildings. A bit like the year 12 parties celebrating the end of high school known as Schoolies Week on the Gold Coast.

It's day six of my adventure, and I'm heading south into a cooler climate; I can already feel the chilly morning dew. The sky is a beautiful dark blue with a golden glow on the horizon. It's time to get up and get back on the road before my fellow campers get the guitar out again.

I manage to get on the road early, but I haven't had coffee or breakfast, so I'm feeling like I've missed out on something. The sun's still low on the horizon as I pass the monument to the drovers and cattlemen who worked this land. The Stockman's Hall of Fame is an impressive place as is the equally impressive QANTAS Museum. It would have been great to stay another day. My plan today was to get to Tambo, home of the famous chicken races and location of the famed "Teddy Bear's Picnic."

In the small town of Ilfracombe, I found a kerbside coffee shop. It's the local hotel that has cut a hole in the wall to provide morning coffee for us early travellers—a great place to stop for a coffee and breakfast. This will provide enough time for the sun to rise and the kangaroos to find a place to sleep for the day.

The road from Ilfracombe to Barcaldine changes from wide-open grassland to shrubbery and then tall eucalypt forests. There was smoke from a fire that was probably the result of some winter burning off; the lack of breeze to blow it away made it hang like fog in the trees and encroach the road silently like a silent menacing fog. The sides of the road are plastered with dead kangaroos, and now and then a sign that warns you to watch out for kangaroos. Maybe they need to make a sign in kangaroo language because the road looks like some mass killing field. It wasn't long before the Barcaldine town sign came into view, just above the dead bodies of a family of kangaroos.

It was here in 1891 that three of the newly formed shearers' unions, three thousand workers and their families came together to protest the poor wages and conditions of shearers, and it is here where the great shearer strike officially started, even though general unrest and militancy was occurring right across the region with strike camps from Cloncurry to the New South Wales border.

A militant group of shearers had taken up arms in Clermont, just down the road, and had joined up with those at Barcaldine to create Australia's second armed uprising. They even marched under the Eureka Stockage flag. History shows that the Eureka Stockade didn't go too well for the miners, and neither did the second uprising for the shearers. It was only luck, not good planning, that prevented the 150 troopers sent to Barcaldine from being overrun, such was the anger the shearers had for the governor of the day. The troops were grossly outnumbered and outgunned. However, there were many families in the crowd, which would have mitigated the anger and prevented a full-scale attack on the troops. However, they managed to arrest the union leaders, who were taken away, tried, and found guilty of sedition.

Even though the authorities didn't realise it at the time, they had inadvertently set the scene for political opposition in Australia, putting one more nail in the coffin of any hope of re-establishing the feudal system in the colonies.

The governor quickly reinforced the Barcaldine troops with 1,000 extra men to take back and secure the railway station. Even though history shows the troopers won this part of the battle, it was nowhere near a victory, and the shearers still had the numbers where it counted. The shearers lost direction after the arrest of their leaders and retreated, only to reform sometime later in other smaller pockets of insurrection, including the burning down of the shearing shed at McPherson's station. They realised they couldn't win by armed conflict, so they got together in the pub to discuss tactics, but there wasn't enough room for everyone, so they crossed the road and sat down under an old gum tree to talk about how they could put pressure on the government of the day. The result was the writing of the labour manifesto and the formation of a political party, this was initially the Queensland Labour Party but soon became the Australian Labor Party with the North American spelling. It is still spelt incorrectly today.

The first time I passed this way was in 2000 when I drove through on my way to a new job in Mount Isa. I remember looking for a place to eat my lunch and finding this old raggedy gum tree to sit under. Little did I know at the time that this raggedy gum tree was the very one those union leaders and shearers sat under back in 1891 to discuss political power and the rights of shearers.

They called the tree "The Tree of Knowledge," and it had folklore status in the ranks of the Labor movement. The "Tree of Knowledge" was a common ghost gum, thought to be over 200 years old when it died. The tree is long dead, and this is where the story gets intriguing. On the 3rd of October 2006, the great "Tree of Knowledge" was proclaimed "murdered."

The rest of that story reads like a Dan Brown novel. There were a number of the usual suspects, Ruben Carter's name was mentioned, Dr Plum from the library, and even John Howard, the Liberal Prime Minister of Australia, was implicated.

An Australian election was imminent, and the tree became a rallying cry for the Labor Party. Having used the poor diseased tree as a martyr, when they got elected they spent over 10 million dollars building a monument to it. I'm sure that is a justifiable use of taxpayers' money.

As I stand looking at the white ghostly stick that is the poor dead "Tree of Knowledge," I can't help thinking, "I wonder what the swaggies and shearers of 1891 would have thought about this monument to their cause." To me, the ghostly remains of that once proud tree, left to stand under a monument of steel and glass, is a travesty. I was fortunate to have sat where the shearers sat under the tree when it was alive; there was shade and a place to put my bag and brew my coffee, and I was amongst nature.

I feel sad; it should have just been buried or even burnt in some sort of ritualised swaggie campfire, where people could talk and laugh and toast a beer to a great old tree. I don't know if it was the breeze in the trees or a ghost from the past, but I heard in my mind the cheering and laughing of a group of guys around a campfire. No sooner had I heard it that it was gone; maybe this is how ghosts talk to us, through our dreams. After wandering around a little bit and reading the sign that tells the story, I got back on Emu and turned south.

Chapter 10
The Birth of Australian Democracy

The next part of my journey today was to take me from the outback to civilisation, and in doing so, visit one of the most recognised old tree stumps in Australia's history. The road to Blackall is a straight line, while most of it is thousands of hectares of Mitchell grass plains, there are forests of eucalypt trees that border the road and line the creek beds. About 40 kilometres out of Blackall, I come across one of those iconic rest areas. Set amongst large ghost gums and other eucalypts, an old concrete table with a wooden shade was off to one side, on the other was a bridge and the Barcoo River. It's a hot day and I'm starting to feel a pain in my butt from the uncomfortable seat. I stop at the concrete table and remove my riding jacket, helmet, and gloves. It feels good to wander around between the trees and check out the bridge over the mighty Barcoo River.

The Aboriginal name Barcoo means "dividing country belonging to two tribes." The Barcoo River serves as a boundary between two Aboriginal groups of the region. In the Guwa language, the term Barracoo means "big river or large creek." The Barcoo River, like all the rivers in this region, flows inland to Lake Ayr in central

Australia. A distance of about 2,500 kilometres from where I'm currently sitting.

During heavy wet seasons, the Channel Country lives up to its name as all the creeks flood. If you are lucky enough to be able to fly over the channel country during these times, you can see the head of the water column, where the land is stark and dry in front of the water and it gets progressively greener and lusher behind it. However, on this day it was dry and a perfect place to camp. But my goal was to get to the famous chicken races in Tambo and it was far too early to pull up for the night.

There's a myth that Australians will bet on which of two flies will fly off the wall first, such is our fascination with gambling. Another great Australian outback pastime is called the Barcoo Wave. Without realising it, I was becoming very adept at the famous Barcoo Wave, a technique to swat away the millions of flies that just appear from nowhere. I understand there's a competition and a betting system for the most flies swatted in an hour. Why am I not surprised?

Getting back on Emu, it wasn't long before I arrived in Blackall. It is situated at the junction of the famous Barcoo River, and the Landsborough Highway. It has two famous landmarks, the "Black Stump" and a monument to its most famous son, "Jacki Howe."

Arriving in Blackall, I find myself in a typical Queensland country town, but this is more than just your average country support centre. This is, in fact, the boundary of civilisation as we know it. On one side of town is the sophisticated urban arena, while on the other the ravages of an uncivilised, untamed wilderness. Interestingly, the school is on the untamed side, and while I appreciate the dichotomy, I can't see any difference in the town's architecture from one side to the other.

In the early times of exploration, stumps were used by surveyors to set up their equipment. This stopped the equipment from sinking into soft or damp ground. The original term "Black Stump" came out of a land dispute in New South Wales (NSW). The term "Outback" referred to the land "Outback" of the survey marker at the old "Black Stump."

The "Outback" statement was first used for this legal argument in a court case. A grazier was complaining about a squatter who had set up a sheep race on his property allocation. The squatter argued the land did not belong to the grazier because it was "Outback of the Black Stump" and therefore not possibly within the grazier's land allocation. From that case, it became synonymous with the known or surveyed civilised area and the unknown not yet surveyed and uncivilised area. The black stump was where the "Outback" officially started.

However, there are many black stumps in the Australian bush, but only three claim to be the actual "Black Stump" that defines the dichotomy between civilisation and the "Outback." The three black stumps can be found in Blackall (QLD), Coolah (NSW), where the original court case was heard, and Merriwagga (NSW).

I find it interesting the "Black Stump" used by surveyors in 1887 in Blackall was burnt down and had to be replaced. It was already a black stump, presumably being a tree that had burnt down in the first instance before being used as a survey marker. Otherwise, I guess it would have been a tree, which would not have the same connotation or practical use. So important was the Black Stump to Queensland and Blackall's history that the town replaced it with a statue of a black stump in 2018. The stump was not as important to the Labor Party as the Tree of Knowledge; otherwise, the monument would have been much grander.

Even though cattle play a big role in the agricultural community around Blackall, it is sheep that first motivated Europeans to venture out here. It is sheep that make the town famous. In this region, there are legendary stockmen and women, and no one was more legendary than the great "Jacki Howe."

Much of the past couple of days riding was through sheep country, although I'm not sure if this is just a myth as I haven't seen any. Sheep were so important to early Europeans that the country was said to be prospering off the "sheep's back". Demand for wool from the colonies was bringing solid prices worldwide and Blackall was front and centre in this trade.

For many people in the cities at the time, all they knew about the "Outback" was that it was uncivilised and the home of sheep stations and hostile Aboriginals. In Queensland, gun shearers were like modern rock stars and no one was faster or better than Jackie Howe, who in 1892 sheared 321 sheep in 7 hours and 40 minutes, a record that was only beaten in 2015. Jackie Howe used hand shears.

I had finally come to the heart of old Australia and the heartland of the swaggie. It was here and places like this dotted around the country where the quintessential Australian character was formed and where the hard-working, beer-drinking, and semi-militant Aussie battler came from.

While I rode around town and soaked in the history of this place, I could only stop long enough for lunch before having to hit the road again, if I was going to get to Tambo before the kangaroos came out and the sun retired for another day.

My motorcycle tour of outback Queensland was now officially over. I had found what it meant to be a swaggie, uncovered the truth of the murdered swaggie at the combo waterhole, and found his heartland. Hopefully, having published the truth, the ghost can lay to rest. I'm no longer on an outback motorcycle tour of Queensland. I've crossed over and I'm now in the civilised part of Queensland.

As I ride out of Blackall, past the "Black Stump" and onto Tambo, I lament on all that I have learnt so far. I've always thought that Outback and Regional Queensland were a place of honesty and hard work. Nothing I had come across so far could detract me from that thought, except maybe another chorus of kumbaya.

Tonight, I get to make my fortune at the world-famous chicken races. I'll enjoy a couple of red wines as I toast the swaggie and his role in creating the Australia we have today and thank him for his efforts.

Chapter 11
International Chicken Racing

Last night, I bit the bullet (metaphorically) and spent the night in a motel room. It was the first time I had stayed in a motel on this journey. I'm not sure how I felt about it. For some reason, I miss the early morning ritual of rolling off my camp stretcher, stumbling up on my knees, getting my arm caught on the tent fly as I squeeze out of my tent, and landing flat on my face.

So after two long days on the road, I thought a good night's sleep would help alleviate some of the fatigue I had built up. At the same time, there was an international race event happening at the local pub, so making sure I was clean and presentable was paramount. The world-famous chicken racing circuit was in Tambo, so I decided to take a look and hopefully make my fortune on chickens.

My mother had been an amateur chicken breeder most of her life and I had grown up with chickens as a kid. How hard could it be to pick a winning chicken with all that inherited knowledge? It was fortuitous that the stadium was opposite my motel at The Royal Carrangarra Hotel. Maybe this is why I had packed to meet the Queen; it was billed as a rival to the famous Melbourne Cup or even Royal Ascott.

In Australia, there is a culture of betting on everything that moves, from flies on the wall to yabbies at the local river, usually in the confines of the local pub. The problem with betting on flies in the outback is that there are so many of them and they all look the same, sorry if you think this is racist but it's a fact. The problem is you have to keep your eyes on them to know which one won the race—when you're trying to collect your winnings there's usually a big argument as to whose fly it was that won. Seriously, betting on flies is a mug's game. Chickens, on the other hand, can be sprayed with coloured powder without actually killing them in the process (unlike flies).

Dinner was to be at the Royal Carrangarra Hotel. It was also the home of Ben's Chicken Racing circuit. This quote from Ben's website says it all: "The most ridiculous and entertaining thing I have ever seen. Chicken Racing, who would have thought!"

Having taken my time washing some clothes and having a shower, I got to the bar just as the chickens were finishing their first race. I was keen to order a pub meal and was told if I wanted to order before the races were completed, I should have done so before 5:30 pm. It was now 5:40 pm and I was out of luck and destined to wait. I grabbed a schooner of ale and headed out back to participate in the racing activity.

I thought that such an important royal occasion warranted a verse from my favourite poem, so after selecting my chicken sculling my beer, I penned the following:

"All the chickens had gathered at the fray for the word had got around that the chick from Old Regret was in the line."

There was Grettle showing metal, Florence from the Lower Lawrence, and Maisy from Mount Daisy,

The runt of the pack was Old Flew who was painted Black and Blue,

Bob said he warranted that Flew would be there at the end.

Not quite the "Man from Snowy River," but still befitting the event, I thought. This was reassuring, so I wagered my 10 dollars on old Flew and I was now ready for the off. The chicken races were spectacular and not for the faint of heart. Unfortunately, my chicken-picking abilities correspond to my horse-picking ability in my once-yearly bet on the Melbourne Cup and I ended up donating a lot of money to the Royal Flying Doctor service. I was heartened by the fact that it is a worthwhile cause and one that provides a lifeline for outback communities.

I decided then and there that chicken racing was almost as pointless as betting on flies and was not going to make me rich. I retired to the line of people in the main bar ordering dinner. I decided it was only appropriate to order chicken parmigiana. More than likely, it was the poor chicken who ran last in each race (my chicken). I did notice some strange blue powder on the side of the plate. I guess you have to be tough to survive in the regions, a clear case of survival of the fittest, or in this case, the fastest.

The second famous attraction at Tambo is that it is home to the Tambo Teddy Bear, and rumour has it, the location of the Teddy Bear's Picnic. This is yet to be confirmed by empirical research, but the evidence that teddy bears are in charge of the town is everywhere.

There is a teddy bear shop that only sells teddy bears. Unfortunately, it was too early for me to acquire my own Tambo

Teddy Bear, which would have been a great mascot for my motorcycle tour. I had to leave town early because I had a long and technical ride ahead of me today.

After packing my gear onto Emu and securing it, I rode around to the front office to drop off the key. In one of the front units, I ran into Dave and Emma. This was the couple I met just outside Longreach when I was taking a break on the concrete table.

They were taking a quick outback spin through the outback in preparation for a ride around Australia. Both were experienced riders and awesome people. It just goes to show the depth of bikers in Australia. What surprised me the most about this couple was their choice of motorcycles. Emma was riding a Harley Davidson Road King, while Dave had a Yamaha FJR 1300. Talk about the odd couple. Up until six months ago, they both toured on Suzuki Boulevards and had decided to upgrade their bikes for the big Aussie road trip.

While Dave was in Adelaide on business, he had wandered into the local Yamaha shop and fell in love with the FJR1300, buying it on the spot and shipping it back to Queensland. At the same time, Emma had visited the Harley dealership and done the same thing with the Road Glide, thinking Dave would buy a similar bike when he got back. They didn't tell each other, until the bikes arrived. The only gripes Emma has is the low suspension and its lack of travel, vibration, and noise (which is why you buy a Harley in the first place). Still, she said she would rather put up with that and have the cruiser seating position anytime. Dave just smiled as all good husbands should. They were going to stay in town and pick up some Tambo Teddies for the grandchildren and Emma was going to edit her drone video footage for the family. They were then heading to St George for the night before heading home to Toowoomba.

Throughout my tour, I have met the friendliest people. There's definitely a shared camaraderie with travellers out here. I wished them safe travels and managed to find a bakery next to a petrol station where I could fuel up with pie and hot coffee, and petrol for Emu.

Chapter 12
Mastering the Wilderness Way

There are four ways to leave Tambo: back to Balcaldine, east over the Dawson Development Road to Springsure, south to St George, or through the Wilderness Way to the western side of the Canarvon Gorge. I planned to ride the 230 kilometres of black soil, clay mud, and sand that constitute the Wilderness Way.

I pulled up at the visitor centre on the edge of town and walked inside. I wanted to learn about the track conditions and book a campsite at the Salvator Rosa camping area within the national park. The friendly young girl at the counter showed me the circuit and gave me a map. There was another man at the counter who was also going that way in his four-wheel drive. We would pass each other in a continuous game of cat and mouse throughout the day and now and then stop at an interesting landmark and have a coffee together.

I got back on Emu and we headed south until I found the road mentioned by the young lady at the visitor centre. The tar seal continues for another 10 kilometres before turning to gravel and then clay. The road starts to climb as you near a large sandstone escarpment, for some time you climb up and twist around giant obelisk-type rock formations before you are given a view of the National Park below. As I rode closer to the National Park, the road turned to a deep red clay, which made riding smooth, at least until I came across some road works. It wasn't long after riding past a grader and a water truck making road repairs that the road became so wet I was finding it difficult to ride. Standing on the pegs, I would counter-steer as the back wheel would slide into the table drain. I would accelerate out and almost do a full 360-degree spin before getting some grip and moving forward again. Eventually, the road dried enough to get reasonable traction and I was able to pick up speed.

The Wilderness Way is one of the most spectacular tracks in Queensland. It dips and twists through sandstone valleys, past cattle properties, and over massive escarpments that provide beautiful scenic views. I found my abilities stretched and my riding out of control when coming down twisty sand-covered hills and trying to stop or navigate the deep sand at the bottom. More than once I twisted up only to miraculously find my way through without falling off.

After three hours of sand, mud, clay, and wet slippery black soil roads, the type of riding tracks that adventure riders love, I finally arrived at the entrance to the national park. A small sign on the locked gate said it all: "Park Closed" and "Burning-off Activities in Progress."

I was disappointed. Salvator Rosa was a gem in Queensland's scenic landscape and a difficult place to get to. It wasn't a place you could come and see for a long weekend adventure; it was a place you had to plan to get to. I guess it just becomes another item in my bucket to be ticked off sometime in the future. To make it worse, there had been no mention of burning off at the information centre.

It was now two-thirty in the afternoon, and time to consider a place to camp for the night. Most of the area was cattle grazing land and very few secluded areas to set up a tent. My only option was to ride towards Springsure on the bull dusty Dawson Development Road. I said goodbye to my new friends and headed east.

They waited for me at the turnoff back to Tambo and we waved goodbye as they turned left, while I veered to the right. About an hour later, I arrived at the junction between the Dawson Development Road and the Wilderness Way. Several "three-dog cattle trucks" went past, dust covering the nearby trees, and slowly filtering towards me like an encroaching fog.

It was three-thirty in the afternoon when I found myself sitting at a small rest area almost on the road at the intersection of the Wilderness Way and the Dawson Development Road. Taking my time to unload Emu, I made a cup of coffee and ate a couple of muesli bars.

After my coffee, I stretched my legs by taking a walk around the rest area. There is a small monument to Major Mitchell's fourth exploration of this area. Mitchell originally surveyed this area in 1841 when looking for great but poorly organised explorers Burke and Wills.

On his fourth exploration in 1848, he came out to follow the water courses and locate possible agricultural land. He discovered a spring-fed creek and named the area Salvator Rosa after the famous European landscape artist of the sixteenth century. After finding and naming the spring, he and his team followed the creek until it joined up with the Barcoo River. This exploration opened up the central west area to sheep and cattle grazing.

It wasn't long before settlers hungry for land swarmed over the area, claiming large parts of it for themselves. It's no wonder there were conflicts between the local Aboriginal tribes who had differentiated tribal boundaries that had been operating successfully for thousands of years and white settlers who seemed oblivious to this claim to the lands.

The Dawson Development Road joins Tambo to Springsure; it's cattle country and during trucking season the road gets pretty beaten up. Graders fix the road at the end of the season, which was about now. I had no idea what the road would be like.

I had about one and a half hours until I got to Springsure. The road was generally good and enabled me to get up to about 90 kilometres per hour in most of the straights. I had started to relax into the flow of the road when all of a sudden, I crested a jump up to reveal about 80 metres of bulldust track.

If you've never encountered bulldust, then it's hard to describe the sheer terror patches of superfine powder like dust can engender. If you think of fine sand and how difficult this can be to ride and then multiply that by ten, you get the picture. But the real problem with bulldust is not sinking deep into it and losing control of your front wheel; it's that you never know how deep it is and if it is hiding sharp edges, uneven side walls, or rocks that can all conspire to throw you off your bike. I have seen camper trailers flip over when being towed through bulldust.

Before I knew it, I was deep in the fine dust that hides deep holes and trenches, my front wheel was flipping around causing me to struggle to control the handlebars as I hit a deep trench and the front wheel dived only to be rescued by a rock that pushed the front wheel out into clear air, jarring my body at the same time. I knew if I let it sink into the dust it was all over and it would throw me off balance and twist the bike. I would end up high-siding the bike with unknown consequences.

I stood on my pegs and wrestled with the front wheel, keeping it in line and accelerated. This behaviour is counterintuitive; all I wanted to do was hit the brakes and make it all stop. Coming into this stretch, I had my weight on the front of the bike, which made the problem worse. Added to that, my tool cases were hanging from the engine protection bars, further increasing the weight over the front wheel.

Once out of immediate danger, I slowed down and took a more considered approach to coming over a jump-up. I decided I needed more weight on the back and to drive more aggressively through the dust and corrugations. As I came upon my next section, I braked heavily in a straight line and engaged the back shock and spring by pulling back on the bike. When I hit the dust, I accelerated while riding the back brake until I had a clear line, powering out of the bulldust at which point I released the back brake.

This happened time after time and always in the most unexpected places. By the time I reached the tar-sealed road some 20 kilometres out of Springsure, I was exhausted. There was a turn-off that said "Minerva National Park," which I thought might have a clear and secluded spot to camp, so I turned left and headed into the park.

If I'm camping in rest areas or a place I shouldn't, I like to make my campsite as stealthy as possible. I would rather hide than have to explain myself. My campsite today was one of those types of camps. I had found some great places but most were exposed to the road and tracks.

One of the great joys of my motorcycle touring is the ability to find sites that suit a small camping setup. It's easy to camp out of the way when there is just you.

After riding around, I managed to find a secluded site on the edge of a cliff. Once I had set up my camp, I kicked back, took off all my riding gear and sat with my legs over the edge of the cliff looking down at the town of Springsure. My tent is tucked away under a small overhang on a rocky platform, and Emu is secured under a hoodie for the night, camouflaged from the road and protected with a brake lock alarm on the handlebar. I contemplated the beauty of life, as I watched the sunset and the sky changing from bright red to an inky black. Down below, I watched the small dots of light flicker on in the town of Springsure.

Looking over the cliff, I can see kangaroos grazing on the grasses below, an eagle is circling high in the sky, looking for her last meal. It's getting dark and the sun is setting as she dives to the ground to pick up some previously contented mouse or kangaroo rat that also had dinner plans that night. Life is meant to be simple unless you happen to be a kangaroo rat or a mouse. So why have humans made it so fucking complicated? Why are so many people stressing all the time? Then I heard the slow methodical beat of a favourite tune, the same one I was listening to in my hammock so long ago now; it was distant at first, but grew as I focused inwardly.

Sittin' in the morning sun

I'll be sittin' when the evening comes

Watching the ships roll in

Then I watch 'em roll away again, yeah

I'm sittin' on the dock of the bay

Watchin' the tide roll away, ooh

I'm just sittin' on the dock of the bay

Wastin' time

That's it, "Dock of the Bay" by Otis Redding. The meaning was suddenly clear to me. In my twenties, I had thought it was a call to adventure. All the memories of that time of my life come flooding back. It's funny that the memories, smells, tastes, and even the vibe of the old pub come flooding back; it was like I was there only yesterday. At the time it typified for me, freedom and not worrying about the world, life was simple, fun, and carefree. Now I realise it was a warning, a new meaning was forming in my mind. One that I had thought about but hadn't articulated. This warning was that if I don't take action, life will drift by and I will be an observer in life, not a participant. Achieving my bucket list items that have been there for years was one way of taking action. The other was to decide to take a solo motorcycle tour around Queensland.

It was here now on this cliff that I realised what Smilie in the movie *City Slickers* meant when he held up his finger. The one thing in all the world I was looking for at this point in my life was freedom. Freedom from stress, from having to be something, from turning up at work and fiddling with staplers. Freedom from being someone I didn't want to be. The movie *Braveheart* now makes sense as Mel Gibson raises his giant sword in the air and shouts down the English army, "Freedom!"

There are all sorts of freedoms: financial freedom, freedom to work when you want, freedom to choose a career, and freedom to sit quietly listening to music or to ride a motorcycle around the world. But I think it is the freedom of the soul that's the most precious.

Chapter 13
Murderous Conflict

"It always rains on tents. Rainstorms will travel thousands of miles, against prevailing winds for the opportunity to rain on a tent."
— Dave Barry

I opened my eyes. It was dark and the trees were rustling. I thought I heard footsteps in the gravel above my tent. That was ridiculous considering where I was. It was too early to get up and begin my trip to Carnarvon Gorge, so why was I awake? I heard a tap on my tent and I froze. There was somebody out there. Then a second tap, and a third. Then a chorus of taps. It became a melody of heavy splattering of giant raindrops on my tent. I breathed a sigh of relief—it was only raining or was it the famed Drop Bear pissing on my fly. Either way, I didn't want to put my head out of the tent. Day eight of my adventure was just about to begin. I unzipped the fly screen slightly and looked out through blurry eyes. There was a hint of the sun, or at least it would be in about three hours when the sun came up in earnest.

On one side was a small rock face, on the other about a metre from the edge of the tent was a 100-metre drop off the side of a cliff. As I am now on the eastern side of the black stump in

Blackall, I am officially no longer in the outback and I was about to begin my new "regional" motorcycle tour of Queensland.

I will ride around the northern and eastern sides of the Carnarvon Gorge National Park and head to arguably the centre of cattle grazing country, but not just yet. I close my eyes and listen to the rain and wind as it pummels my tent. I'm grateful to have secured the tent to all the available trees and rocks. There are seven stakes in the tent base, all seemed to be holding nicely.

This is the first time I am grateful for picking a four-season tent with a nylon fly. When stretched tight, the fly acts to strengthen the tent and I feel quite secure. All seemed well and I drift back to sleep.

When I finally managed to get out of bed, I wandered half-awake to the edge of the cliff and looked down the sheer 100-metre drop. For a second, it didn't register and then it hit me. You know how you get that feeling that runs like electricity up your back and out through your head when you're standing at a handrail on the veranda of a large building? It's strange how it can wake you up from your leisurely slumber to instant awareness. My heart was beating much too fast.

"Shit," I said to myself. Well, it was more like "fucking holy duck shit!" That was close. For a few seconds there I did a fairly accurate impression of a cat on a hot tin roof. I edged back from the cliff and sidled around my tent until I found my chair, table, and cooking gear, which luckily had been stowed in the back vestibule out of the wind and rain.

The sun was well and truly up by the time I had packed and I had managed to get back on the road. I was amazed at how rough the tracks in this area were and I had an interesting time manoeuvring Emu out of his rock-enclosed parking lot. As

I rode back down the rough rock-strewn track, it was early in the morning, the track was a dark brown colour with large grey rocks poking out everywhere, edged by a multitude of green shrubbery and large eucalypt trees.

Kangaroos and wallabies were all over the road and in the grassy areas before the shrubs. It was a magnificent animal refuge. I rode slowly, enjoying the scenery and not wanting to startle the kangaroos. They were too intent on chewing on dry grass to even notice my presence; a simple sideways tilt of the head was all that I got before going back to devouring their grassy treats.

Apart from cattle, Central Queensland has lots of wildlife, from kangaroos to dingoes, foxes, pigs, snakes, brolgas, emus, and lizards of all sorts. This is not to mention some of the awesome bird life that congregates around every dam or available watercourse.

Once I got down the escarpment to Springsure, I was in a very familiar area. My wife's family own and run a cattle property that borders the Carnarvon Gorge National Park. I am heading there for the next couple of days to catch up with them, and do a bit of maintenance on Emu.

It had been over 300 kilometres from Tambo, up the Wilderness Way and into Springsure, so I had to find a petrol station. The BP on the way out of Springsure also offers hot coffee and nutritional highway food. I grabbed a coffee, pie, and chips. Yep, I can hear you now—meal of champions and adventure riders. What else would you eat when there's no bakery in town?

Springsure has an interesting early history. It was initially surveyed by Ludwig Leichhardt in 1845 who identified the rich black clay soil and abundant water from the Comet River. There was a rush to settle in 1859 and it was gazetted as a town in 1863.

Springsure is noted for being the site of one of the biggest massacres of Europeans by an Aboriginal group in Australian history. The Aboriginal Kairi warriors attacked and killed 19 settlers in a place called Cullin-la-ringo.

It's not surprising that conflict broke out in this area. It was reported that Aboriginal warriors stole 300 sheep and in retribution, Aboriginal "Native" police committed rape and other atrocities on the local Aboriginal community. The authorities did nothing to stem this abuse. This was one of many conflicts that were breaking out between Aboriginals and European settlers in the 1880s.

The ride out of Springsure towards Rolleston is some of the best highway riding I've done so far. The morning air is crisp and cool and I find myself weaving around corners and over escarpments, before dropping down the plateau through eucalypt forests onto the vast black soil grassy plains.

The tar-sealed road has sharp uprises and depressions in the surface caused by heavy trucks and hot roads, which during summer can melt. The road has been laid across a black soil plain. Black soil is very fertile and holds water, meaning the road easily buckles. It's not unusual to see power poles perched at different angles along the road. About halfway to the nearest town you ride across the Rolleston Mine rail bridge before going over the incredibly bumpy road that skirts the Comet River overflow. Not only is this excellent grazing land but below the land are large coal deposits and substantial gas reserves. In a car, this road is torturous as it is full of up jumps and bumps, but on a bike, it's quite a pleasant ride. The long travel springs and off-road shocks take the bumps in their stride.

Eventually, I come to a tee intersection. Turning left I ride into the small town of Rolleston, turn right and continue to Carnarvon Gorge and Injune. I take the right turn and ride for about 40 kilometres on the tar before turning right again to go down a dirt-access road known as the Rewan Road. The Rewan Road intersects with the Carnarvon Access Road at the Rewan Station. There's no fuel between Rewan and Injune, which is about 150 kilometres, so if you're going to the Carnarvon Gorge for a visit, you will need at least a 300-kilometre range on your bike. I have over 350 before I hit reserve. I carry a five-litre fuel container, and all up I can comfortably ride for 450 kilometres if needed.

Chapter 14
Cattle Country

I'm familiar with this road and by the time I get here, I know I'm not far from my destination. Instinctively, I relax to enjoy the ride. It's a road I've driven thousands of times and I know every cattle grid and sweeping corner. I also know this is probably the worst time to relax on a bike.

The road is sandy and pitted with potholes and the grass on the side of the road is quite high. Cattle are everywhere, wandering across the road at their leisure. This road, like many in the area, are old stock routes. Stock routes don't belong to anyone and are there for the free movement of cattle. In the old days, graziers would drive cattle to railheads through these lanes, but now they are used as extra feed areas.

The grids separate each paddock and by extension the boundary of each property, with the road often dividing paddocks. All sorts of animals use the stock routes, from emus, to pigs, and dingos. I've also seen plenty of brown snakes skating across the road trying to avoid certain death at the hands of ute-driving ringers who don't have sympathy for these venomous creatures. The kangaroos are thick and fast in this area. I have hit several roos on this road in the past. Lucky for me, I have a bull bar on my ute. Not so lucky for the kangaroo, of course.

I'm feeling more vulnerable now as I take it slower than I usually would. My eyes are scanning like one of the Cylons from the movie *Battle Star Galactica*. It's not long before the towering sandstone monolith of Mount Carnarvon comes into view. This is the eastern boundary of my in-law's cattle property. I am especially vigilant on this section as I believe my father-in-law is secretly breeding kangaroos. There seems to be more in this area than any other part of the Carnarvon Gorge. Coincidence? I think not.

This region is blessed with some of the most stunning scenery in Queensland, and is often referred to as the "Rooftop of Queensland." There is a massive amount of biodiversity in the area. I've talked to people who have never been this far out into the regions and I always get the same response.

"Oh, the farmers don't care about the environment. They just kill the land, knock down trees, and cause global warming." But nothing I have seen can be further from the truth. Sure, land has been cleared in the past, but if it hadn't, many people would go hungry today.

The biodiversity in the region puts the average suburban city to shame, not to mention the number of cars that spend most of their morning and afternoon pumping out carbon monoxide while waiting at traffic lights. Much of the commentary is misdirected. Graziers and landholders have a vested interest in having a healthy property; it's an absolute must if you want to run a profitable business out here.

It was the middle of winter and by the time I got to the creek that runs through the property, the sun was starting to go down. I would have time to catch up with the family and put Emu to bed in one of the machinery sheds. It was a strange feeling riding past the cattle yards and into the main housing area. I hadn't ridden my bike here before and rarely was I here by myself. After a medium-cooked steak, vegetables, and a few glasses of red wine, it was time for bed.

In the morning, I just lay in bed, thinking about my journey so far and what I have discovered about myself. There's a great quote from Robert Pirsig's book, *Zen and the Art of Motorcycle Maintenance*, which says:

The place to improve the world is first in one's own heart and head and hands and then work outward from there. Other people can talk about how to expand the destiny of mankind. I just want to talk about how to fix a motorcycle. I think that what I have to say has more lasting value.

I can see the sunlight through the trees out the back of the house, just beyond the five, ten-thousand-litre water tanks. The sun is mottled by the giant gum trees that stand sentinel along the banks of the creek. The country scenery is in strong contrast to my normal city life. The working dogs locked overnight in their dog boxes are barking for attention. The cockatoos (who, by the way, are much louder than galahs) are squawking incessantly in the cockatoo tree.

While I lie there in bed, snug against the frosty morning, I'm momentarily taking in this country scenery and how different it is from my normal city living. There is a peacefulness that can't possibly be gained from a noisy congested city landscape. No amount of "backward-facing dog" or "warrior" poses in the yoga class can compensate for sitting on the veranda of a rural property with a hot cup of coffee, watching the cattle chomp merrily on the grass.

When you ride solo on a motorcycle, you tend to see the world differently, like a movie where you are part of the action rather than just an observer. People treat you differently, and you join a secret society of brother (and sister) bikers.

Probably the only other people who understand what it means to be a biker and ride in solitude are other solo travellers. Similarly, when you engage with people outside of your cultural groups you have to extend yourself to see the world through their eyes and try not to be blinkered by your own reality. The difference between riding solo and riding with buddies is that, as a solo rider, you have to engage completely with the different peoples.

I have three goals today. First, to rationalise my gear and store some here to be picked up at Christmas time. Second, to do some preventative maintenance. And third, to explore some single tracks and creek crossings.

Early in the morning, I washed Emu and cleaned off eight days of dust and grime. I had now travelled over 4,000 kilometres, about 800 on dirt roads and outback tracks. I had brought a spare air filter covered in oil and decided this was the opportune time to replace the existing one.

The chain needed cleaning and adjustment and I took the opportunity to clean off all the crusted oil and dirt before soaking it in chain lube. I noticed one of the main subframe bolts had disappeared and now that I was thinking of it, it explains some of the tapping noises I had heard on the gravel road from Rolleston. It takes a little while trawling through the spare bolt and nut bin in my brother-in-law's workshop before I find a suitable replacement. I have to cut it down to fit and I put a split washer on the nut to prevent it from undoing by itself.

It's a great day for riding, so I take Emu up the tracks to the top of the property where it borders the national park. The track is through deep eucalypt forests of ghost and spotted gum, climbing high into the surrounding mountains and going through numerous crossings of the creek. As I ride up from the hills and onto the sandy flats, I'm aware of the conspicuously hidden dingo traps. Because of this awareness, I'm even more conscious of not coming off. At one point, I feel the front wheel pull dramatically sideways and counter-intuitively I accelerate, driving the back wheel into the sand and pulling the front wheel up slightly, just enough to correct my course. Some tyres trap the sand and some release it easily; I think I have the first. I'm constantly fighting the front wheel to take the line.

The area is known as Black Alley due to the sharp lava peak that borders the national park. It is a spectacular country and some of the most picturesque scenery in the area. In earlier times, mustering cattle up here was a week-long job. Today, it's a completely different operation. Mustering is usually done with the help of a helicopter and quad bikes. Cattle are held in temporary yards and driven down the track to the main stockyard.

This is the first time I have been able to test out the KLR in single-track conditions. This is the exact reason I bought this bike. I'm not an enduro rider; I like to take my time. Emu handled the track well. If I was choosing a bike to race around the farm, I wouldn't go for a KLR; like all adventure bikes, they're just too heavy.

Likewise, there are much better touring bikes out there that make highway riding more enjoyable. But to have a bike that can do both is an absolute joy.

It was starting to get late in the afternoon and I had about two hours to get back. By the time I rode back past the stockyards, the sun was starting to go down behind the ridge and my father-in-law had a bottle of red chilling in the fridge. Tomorrow, I start day 10 and my journey towards the coast. If I had time, I would have visited the Carnarvon Gorge National Park. It's a 40-kilometre trip down the tar-sealed road to the national parks office. There are several commercial camping grounds in the area and each of them offers a bush camping experience.

If you have time, I would recommend the Carnarvon Gorge Walk as one of the most spectacular in Queensland. The walls of the gorge are steep sandstone monoliths, with the crystal-clear Carnarvon Creek running through it. You can visit the Moss Gardens, the Amphitheatre, or the Rock Art Gallery in a day of activities. I've been to the gorge several times over the years, but as I wanted to meet up with some mates on the Gold Coast, I needed to carry on riding.

Chapter 15
Captain Starlight Was Here

The temperature was below freezing on the veranda as I savoured my morning coffee. I clasped the cup between my freezing hands as steam wafted up. My breath was making clouds of vapour as the hot internal air mixed with the overnight freezing temperatures. The days in Queensland during winter can start cold but as the sky was a deep translucent blue, without a cloud, I knew it was going to be an awesome day of riding. I just had to wait until the sun came up to burn off the frost and to make sure the kangaroos were off the road.

I'm heading to Surat on the Balonne River. This area is where the Murray Darling River system starts. The river is confusing. It starts about 100 kilometres upstream from Surat as the Condamine, eventually becoming the Balonne and then the Darling River. The Darling flows through Queensland and New South Wales until it reaches Wentworth in Victoria and joins the Great Murray River. It then flows through to the mouth in South Australia.

The river provides water for agricultural and environmental purposes. It is a much-needed water supply for inland and remote communities. In Australia's early European history, it was a lifeline for those communities. When the Darling flowed, it allowed river boats to come inland as far as Burke in NSW. It delivered much-needed supplies and took away wool to markets in Victoria and South Australia. It was first discovered by Charles Sturt in 1828 who named it after Sir Ralph Darling, Governor of NSW.

I'm riding from Carnarvon Gorge, through Injune, Roma, and ending in Surrat, where I intend to camp on the banks of the Balonne River—exactly where I'm not sure but I have every faith that I will find a campsite somewhere!

It's 327 kilometres from Carnarvon Gorge to Surat. In a straight line, it's about a three-and-a-half-hour ride. The temperature on the veranda at the moment is minus two degrees Celsius. The grass has the first traces of frost for the season, the cockatoos are in the cockatoo tree making a horrendous noise as usual, and the dogs start to bark as I ride past their cages.

There's a rather large Droughtmaster bull with his lady friends near the creek crossing. He's at least six times my size and full of muscle (no wonder the lady cows like him), if he decided to get angry at me and charge I would have no chance to turn the bike and get out of his way. Bulls can be unpredictable around breeding time, but the bulls generally on this property have been chosen because they are calm, so I feel confident if I ride slowly up to him he will be ok. One of his girlfriends wanders off across the creek and he lazily follows, averting any possible confrontation.

Bulls are powerful animals and I have seen a micky bull (unbranded) charge my brother-in-law's CRF250, lift it off the ground with his horns, and throw it over his head. Mind you, we had just castrated it, so I guess you can't blame it for being pissed.

The access road from the farmhouse back to the Rewan Road is fun to ride, with some potholes, a small creek crossing, and some winding dirt corners that are perfect for small power slides. Emu is lighter than he has been since my trip started. I took the opportunity to leave a significant amount of equipment behind in the guest room for me to pick up at Christmas time when I return. I've also removed the tool packs from the front engine protection bars and put them on the back of the soft panniers. There's more connection with the dirt now and I feel the front is much lighter.

Riding down the dirt Rewan Road, I see some curious wallabies and kangaroos look on, while others bounce across in front of me. Once I get on the tar, there's no more dirt until I get to Harry's Hut on the Sunshine Coast.

It's not long before I come across an old plane wreckage on the side of the road. It's a small picnic area with the wing of a World War Two plane, a monument with a plane engine and a plaque with an inscription. The area is surrounded by magnificent eucalypt trees making for a calming bush scene. To build the monument the locals were able to find the remains of a C-47 Dakota transport plane that crashed in the area during the war. It commemorates a tragic event that took the lives of 14 Australians and five American military personnel. On the 16th of November 1943, a Dakota C-47 transport was caught in a ferocious electrical storm over Rewan Station and disintegrated in mid-air.

The plane was travelling from Cloncurry to Archerfield when it went down, and no one survived. The monument was organised by locals as a sign of respect. I can't help but bow my head and thank them silently for their service. I hope we never forget the sacrifice these men made all those years ago.

Just past the monument, the road drops down into a causeway over the Carnarvon Creek. It's a fast-flowing creek and can be quite deep during heavy rain. It's only up to the edge of Emu's tyre, but I take no chances on the slippery concrete and make sure I ride the high side. The drop off the causeway is about one and a half metres and I don't like the idea of having to walk back to my parents-in-law and ask them to borrow the tractor.

It takes about 20 minutes to ride through Rewan Station to the Carnarvon Highway. I turn right at the tee intersection and gun the engine. Emu is purring at about 110 kilometres per hour and I'm sitting just under 5,000 revs per minute. The road is a good stretch of bitumen that runs through kilometre after kilometre of cattle grazing grassland. But it's not long before I start to climb up through the tail of the Carnarvon National Park and onto a plateau.

The road turns and twists and becomes narrower in places, and a large cattle truck rumbles towards me. I have no alternative but to wash off speed and get off the road. Occasionally, I drop down off the plateau and into a valley, which seems to have avoided any clearing. It gets colder as the sun disappears behind a sandstone escarpment. The scenery is stunning with bottle trees and a variety of forested vegetation in the valley areas. It's not long until the small town of Injune comes into view. Injune is the gateway to the southwestern section of the Carnarvon National Park. Some tracks take you around the western side of the park. They eventually join up with the Wilderness Way and Salvator Rosa. I understand that it's very sandy and if you intend to ride it you will need to take additional fuel.

Injune is a small country town 88 kilometres north of Roma in the Maranoa District of Queensland. It is best known for its proximity to Carnarvon Gorge. Established on a cattle property, surveyed in 1858, it now supports the travelling tourist market. It is the last fuel stop before Rolleston, which has many visitors fuelling up on their way to Carnarvon Gorge.

Amongst the new shops and cafes are relics of the past which are on display, including an old blacksmith's shop. When I originally came through this town over 30 years ago, it was almost a ghost town with a single petrol station. It's amazing how tourism has revitalised the area.

The sight of a bakery was a welcome relief. I pull up and back Emu into a park between two big polished Land Cruisers. Opposite me are two more giant vehicles connected to equally giant caravans. The ritual of taking off my helmet, gloves, and glasses seems to confuse some people and they look twice at me as I walk past.

There are older people on the veranda, some talking in small groups, others as couples look up momentarily and then look away, All of them seemingly wealthy, judging people by their clothes and jewellery.

I nod at them and give them a friendly smile, but strangely they look away again and continue their conversation. No one acknowledges me. Even at the counter, there's no friendly smile from those waiting to order. For the first time in my outback trip, I feel a coldness from people. I shake it off and find a seat between two groups, but I get the feeling that I'm invisible to these people. Not that this bothers me at all; I have long got over what other people think of me. So I slurp my coffee and eat my chips.

It's not long before I'm back on the road again. Just as I leave town, another biker rides past. I give a courteous wave and he returns the gesture. The cold unpleasantness lifts as I ponder being back amongst my kind again. With a full stomach, I relax and enjoy the countryside as it changes from a forested area back into grazing land. Previously, this road was just cattle trucks and country utes. Today, it's caravans, motor homes, and camper trailers. There's the occasional tourist bus and very occasional biker. As the countryside becomes sparser, signs appear, advertising plumbing supplies and motel accommodation. It's not long until the outer limits of the town of Roma come into view.

What the fuck? A traffic light. It's the first traffic light I have come across since leaving home 10 days ago. Isn't it amazing that there are some things you don't miss? The town is bustling with traffic, from traditional country utes, to expensive Land Cruisers, and even an assortment of mining cars with their yellow warning lights on top and their big "Dukes of Hazard" numbers on the side.

One of the first things I noticed about Roma, apart from its traffic congestion and the traffic lights, is the bulging Queensland bottle trees. These trees look so much like the Boab Trees found in the Kimberley that it's uncanny. I was amazed at how big and industrious the town had become in the five years since my last visit. It is booming with all manner of road works, town bypasses, and the development of industrial estates.

The town was named after Lady Diamantina Bowen (Contessa Diamantina di Roma), wife of Sir George Bowen, first Governor of Queensland. It was gazetted as a town in 1867. For much of its life, it has been the central location for the western cattle industry, but today, it is also known for its natural gas supply.

One of the earliest crops in this region was grapes. Now, that surprised me as I thought grapes were only grown in the cooler climates down south. As it turns out, Roma has a perfect climate for growing grapes and an enterprising man called Samuel Symons Basset first brought cuttings to the region in 1877 and established the Romavilla Winery.

This is by far one of the longest-running businesses in the Maranoa area, having a history from 1877 until around 2012 when it was sold out of the Basset family after floods damaged the winery. It is currently closed and there is no indication if it will re-open for business.

I remember stopping and buying the token bottle of port from the cellar door about 20 years ago. Even though I didn't like the port, it is still sad to think the business lasted so long and then had to close because of the weather.

There are a couple of sayings in the beef industry, "Never kill and eat your cattle as they never taste as good as your neighbour's". Sometimes fences break and cattle disappear. Technically, this is called "Cattle Duffing" (stealing) and as you can imagine it's a criminal act. The reason I'm contemplating this is because I just happened to pull up opposite the Roma Court House, which has a bit of a checkered history and was the scene of some interesting decisions. Its most famous case was that of the infamous cattle duffer (thief), Captain Starlight, who was tried and acquitted of cattle duffing in 1873, even though there was significant evidence that he did commit the crime. The captain's real name was Frank Pearson but he took the name of Captain Starlight from the Rolf Boldrewood novel, *Robbery Under Arms*, when he became what was called a "bush ranger" or, in England, they would have been known as a "highwayman" (thief). When considering what happened to the Aboriginal warriors in Springsure and the poor swaggie at the combo waterhole, it's not hard to think that it was an unjust country back in the late 1800s.

As the story goes, Frank Pearson was one of those blokes who couldn't lie straight in bed and had not only many aliases but a reputation as a murderer. It is believed that he had murdered a cop in a shootout in a pub somewhere in NSW. He served 15 years for the murder, having had his sentence reduced due to some family connections.

It's about 80 kilometres from Roma to Surat. After picking up a new gas canister and some food at the local supermarket, I pull out onto the main street and head east before turning south to Surat.

As I ride out of town, I'm reminded of the true nature of this town. There are gigantic cattle yards with big three-dog road trains. These massive trucks are waiting to pick up and transport cattle to the local abattoirs.

There are acres of dry brown Mitchell grass flats as far as the eye can see. After about half an hour, the topology changes to low-lying shrubbery. Eventually, it starts to turn to forested areas. I arrive at the Balonne River just out of Surat. This is as good a place as any to have lunch, so I take out my travel rations and set my camp stove to boil water for a cup of coffee. The rest area would be a great place to camp. It's a bit dry and dusty and right next to a main road, but there's plenty of room. In one corner, is an old Toyota Land Cruiser with an equally old and rusting caravan. An equally crusty old guy is sitting in the shade on a camper chair watching his dog chew an old bone. I give him a nod of recognition; he nods back. As I sit in the shade of a picnic table, a large road train thunders past, shaking the ground and disturbing the little dog.

It's good to be sitting out enjoying the great Australian bush. I take a small walk over to the bridge and peer down and the shallow creek. When it rains, this becomes a raging torrent, but now is a small brown trickle of water. At least it has water; many creeks at this time of year are bone dry.

The heat of the day is building so it's great to be back on the road. Another 30 kilometres and I can see the signs indicating the impending arrival at the town. I ride past an area that offers free camping by the Balonne River called Fisherman's Rest. There are several vans pulled up already, all within a short distance of a rather large toilet block.

It's early to set up camp, so I ride over the bridge to explore the town first. Surat is a small support town to the grazing industry. There are large cattle trucks either going through town or parked up next to the owner's house. Some of the original buildings have been restored and there is a well-maintained Cobb and Co station in the middle. As I ride around, I see more old buildings having been immaculately restored to their former glory. The council building is a two-story wooden building with red walls and white columns. I've never seen this type of building in a small Queensland town before. It looks very impressive, like being in a living museum.

After riding around the town and checking out the local caravan park, I go back to the Fisherman's Rest area and look for a campsite for the night. The choice of camping areas at Fisherman's Rest is substantial. I'm spoilt for choice. I think about camping down by the river, but I'm concerned about the giant spotted gum trees that are known for dropping three-tonne branches without warning. In the end, I find a nice flat spot behind some large boulders up near the car park. This area is much easier to set up a tent and safer for Emu. Vans and campers are filling up the campground and spreading out in all available spots.

    It's starting to get cold and dew is forming on the tent. I quickly put Emu's camouflage cover on him and start my BioLite stove. The small stove provides a lot of heat and a significant amount of warmth to me as the air gets colder. I could light a bigger fire, there is plenty of firewood and covered fire pits. The BioLite stove is much more fun and easier. I look out over the Balonne River thinking that one day it would be good to traverse this in a kayak.

    I put on my down jacket and woollen hat. It's going to be a cold night. I sit back and feel content with my ride today. The small BioLite fire provides a glow that lights the tent and gives me a small bit of warmth as it flickers and whirrs. My phone is charging from the built-in battery, so I feed the fire a few more sticks and watch the flames dance around. This feeling of freedom and the lack of any need to plan or converse with other people is a feeling that I very rarely experience.

Chapter 16
Fishing in the Outback

"He liked fishing and seemed to take pride in being able to like such a stupid occupation."
— **Leo Tolstoy**, *Anna Karenina*

This is a great place to go fishing. I like fishing, but I'm not very good at it. I'm one of the 90 per cent of people who spend lots of money on fishing gear to never catch fish. I think it's just my way of subsidising friends of mine who do catch fish. Without me and others like me, they wouldn't be able to afford to buy their fishing gear. My camp spot is on the Balonne River just outside of Surat in South West Queensland. Yesterday, I rode from Carnarvon Gorge to Surat, via Injune and Roma. It was an interesting ride and very enjoyable to be heading south into a cooler climate.

Sometime in the middle of the night, I woke up with my teeth chattering—fuck, its cold. I roll around in my down sleeping bag, but no matter what I do, I can't get warm. I sit up, find my down jacket, and try and get back to sleep. I look at my watch and it's three-thirty in the morning. Fuck, I'm getting rid of this bloody air mat as soon as I get home, I vowed to myself.

But it's too late, I'm awake now. So I get up, find my head torch and make my way across to the park's toilets. It's cold, not just cold in the normal sense, but *bloody cold*. The term "bloody cold" is an official rating in the outback. It's in between "Cold minus two degrees Celsius" and "Fucking Freezing at minus 10 degrees Celsius." Once back at the tent, I put my bike jacket over my down jacket and get back into bed. The inflatable mat is not inflated so I pump more air into it and put some more air into my inflatable pillow.

Emu had a great night under his camo cover and managed to keep dry even though you could fill a billy with the amount of water that condensed on the cover. I'm lucky enough to have a watch that tells me the temperature, minus five degrees Celsius. I decided not to start my fire this morning. Instead, I put on my woollen hat and with my hands tucked into my jacket, I made my way across the bridge and along the walking track into town, hoping to find a coffee shop and bakery so I can warm up both inside and out.

As I walk along, I come across several informational signs. One explains how the local Surat Fishing Club stocks the weir. It's not often you think about competitive fishing while touring the roads of South Western Queensland. But in Surat, it's a big deal. Each year, the river is stocked with fingerlings of Murray River Cod, Barramundi, and Yellowbelly. After they mature, there's a competition to catch them again. Interestingly, each of these species is known for being a challenging catch—impossible, in my case.

The town's name, Surat, is synonymous with the basin it resides on. The Surat Basin is famous for its massive coal deposits and, more recently, its significant oil reserves. However, the town's history has been linked to beef production since it was surveyed by Major Mitchell during his fourth expedition to the region in 1846. Established in 1850, Surat has always been a major support hub.

After my exploration, I find a coffee shop and settle in for a warm breakfast, finally escaping the cold. The coffee is large, the kind you can wrap both hands around. I take my time, savouring the coffee as I eat my beef pie. Occasionally, a huge cattle truck rattles through town, a reminder of the region's grazing heritage.

Refreshed, I continue my journey along the walking track. It's still chilly, but the morning sun is burning off the dew and the sky is clear. Mist rises off the water, accompanied by the pleasant sound of flowing water. In the distance, birds call out for their mates. The birdlife here is spectacular, with lorikeets, fantails, magpies, and kookaburras, all seemingly laughing as I pass by. Surat, like many small Queensland towns, sources its water by damming the local river. About two kilometres along the walking track, a small weir is flowing fast, creating clouds of white water—a sight that seems to cleanse the soul.

The Balonne River flows down to St George and then across the border into New South Wales, where it eventually joins the Darling River, which meanders down to the Murray River in Victoria.

After a four-kilometre walk—the longest I've taken on this adventure—I return to my campsite. Many overnight guests are packing up, preparing for their next journey. I do the same, soon hitting the road again. This time, I backtrack slightly and take an adjoining road from Surat to Dalby, then onto Toowoomba for the night.

At a tee intersection, I turn right onto the road to Tara. My outback and regional motorcycle tour is almost complete. I will head into Toowoomba today and then drop down into the Lockyer Valley on my way to the coast. Today, I'm still immersed in regional and country Queensland, so I sit back in my seat and enjoy the view while scanning for kangaroos.

Just as I round a corner, my breath is taken away by the sight in front of me. One of the largest eagles I've ever seen is perched over a small wallaby on the road. Startled, she stretches out her wings and with two powerful thrusts, lifts into the air, wallaby in tow. With another couple of wing pumps, she is climbing higher.

I slow down and pull over to watch the magnificent creature veer left and descend into a paddock about 300 metres away, where she can feast in solitude, undisturbed by the noise of motorcycles. I've seen big eagles before, but the proximity and openness you experience on a motorcycle are breathtaking. By the time, I realise I have a camera and retrieve it from my tank bag, it's too late.

This isn't the first time I've been in awe of Mother Nature on this trip, from the formation flight of cockatiels on the ride to Kynuna to the giant willy-willy on the road to Winton. These experiences are undeniably heightened on a motorcycle.

I've mentioned it before, but for me, these awe-inspiring moments are what I call "Wow" factors. It's hard to describe a Wow factor, but it's akin to an exhilarating rush of amazement, making the world seem magical, and I feel fortunate to witness such events. When I'm feeling down or low on energy, these Wow factors lift my spirits.

The next town I reach is Glen Morgan. It's still early; the streets are void of traffic and people. There's a small grassy area next to an almost deserted petrol station. The grass is long and tinder dry, adding to the eerie ambiance reminiscent of a ghost town. Scattered throughout are rusty cars and trucks, echoing the scenes in Winton. The sign out front reads "A1 Used Cars." I chuckle to myself—what a great sense of humour the owner must have. Then it hits me: when was the last time you saw a 1969 Holden Station Wagon or a 1950s FJ Holden in such condition? These are collector's items, likely worth thousands. I circle back to take another look and snap a photo. The service station, straight out of a 1950s Hollywood movie, would be an ideal backdrop for a Cafe Racing convention, with its classic pop culture design and hand-pumping petrol bowsers. There's definitely a story here, but with it closed and no one around, it's a place to revisit another day. Yet, I can't help but laugh at the scene, imagining the owner's fantastic sense of humour; I'd like to meet him someday.

The towns are starting to get closer together and it's not long until I get to Meandarra, which is about halfway between Surat and Tara. The town is clean and reminiscent of your typical outback community. I pass a sign that says "botanical gardens." For a moment, I contemplate pulling up and finding a quiet place in the gardens to stealth camp. But it's only lunchtime so I continue towards Dalby, I'll stop at Tara for lunch. Tara isn't a major town, it's another support centre and a convenient place to stop. It's about an hour from Dalby and two hours from Toowoomba.

It's a relief to arrive in Tara and I'm starting to feel hungry, so I look around for a place to set up my stove and make a coffee, but there was no park or rest area in town. The only place that had a table and chairs was the small court yard near the library.

I could, of course, go to the pub for a counter meal, but that would probably stretch my budget for today, so I elect to have tuna and rice staple and a cup of coffee.

In a car, I might have just driven through, but on the bike solo I have the time to explore a little, and I need to rest before the next couple of hours riding, which I know will require my complete concentration.

Parts of this town resemble living museums, such as the pub and the old general store. After lunch, I ride around, searching for interesting places to photograph, wondering what else might capture my interest. Nearby, there's a large dam just outside of town, barricaded with no entry signs and red and white tape. In the future, this could be an excellent rest area for travellers like myself. However, for now, it's merely a site of earthworks and machinery. The surrounding tall eucalypts offer a cooling and peaceful escape, yet I must continue my journey. I aim to reach Toowoomba tonight. It's unfortunate that there's no camping spot here; it would be an ideal starting point for my next adventure, especially if I could find a secluded camping area. I'm starting to realise that focusing on reaching a specific destination each night might be detrimental to my mental health and, to some extent, my safety. This focus on the destination, rather than enjoying the journey, detracts from my experiences in the present moment. I wonder if I would find the journey more engaging if I stopped to camp rather than continually riding.

This ride through the agricultural communities in the western parts of Queensland is incredible, offering a glimpse into the life changes since the days of the old stockmen and women, who drove cattle and sheep with horse-drawn carriages. Everywhere in the outback has a connection to the past, with old rusty machinery displayed like proud monuments to a golden era. Yet, I find myself unable to stop and appreciate the smaller points of interest in these communities, so I steer Emu out of town, focused once again on my destination.

Perhaps it's a part of the trap of modern life that we need to be in constant motion, moving to the next position within the company we work for, or simply being upwardly mobile for no particular reason other than to buy more t-shirts from China. Our entire society seems to be perpetually on the move. It's not until you ride these country roads that you realise not everyone is keen on constant movement. Unfortunately, this is a lesson I still need to learn as I head towards the much larger town of Dalby.

Approaching Dalby, the agricultural corporations grow larger, the tractors boast six giant wheels on each side, pulling massive ploughs. This is mass agriculture at its finest, with each property featuring its airstrip, planes parked in formation, and at least two helicopters. This display of real wealth starkly contrasts the smaller properties I've passed over the last few days. Giant irrigation systems extend 200 metres across the fields, spraying water in a continuous stream. These machines, resembling sentinels from another world, make a slow, methodical journey back and forth, day and night, providing a vital lifeline to small tufts of cotton destined to be sent to China for cheap labour to produce more t-shirts. The old, idyllic image of African slaves cheerfully harvesting cotton in the fields, singing "Zip-a-Dee-Doo-Dah," is far from reality and has always been a Hollywood myth.

As I approached Dalby, the landscape transitioned to vast grain farms with a mix of sorghum and wheat, each stretching across about 35,000 acres of flat, cultivated land that seemed to continue to the horizon.

Dalby is a bustling town, serving as a major support centre for the cotton, wheat, and sorghum industries. It's also one of the largest manufacturing hubs for agricultural equipment in Queensland. The total exports from the western Queensland region, including resources and equipment, are estimated at $65.5 billion dollars. Dalby contributes significantly to this with products like agricultural equipment, steel pipes of all sizes, seeders, hydraulic systems, GPS electronics, Clark tanks, plastics, and even the humble "Dingo."

Riding into town, I navigated between large four-wheel drive utes lined up at the local school to pick up children. Trucks rumbled through with empty trailers, ready to transport the next shipment of cattle to the nearby abattoir. It felt chaotic, almost like a scene from "The Wizard of Oz" during the tornado, with cars, trucks, and pedestrians all vying for space. I don't think I took a deep breath the entire time I was there.

Dalby proved to be one of the busiest towns I've encountered, even busier than Roma. I searched for a place to relax, but it was crowded everywhere, with no space to stop and park, even for motorcycles. I eventually found a local weir and a table where I sat for about 30 minutes, but it was hardly relaxing with the constant noise of cars, children, and the loud whistles of truck air brakes.

In my early teaching career, I had worked in Dalby when it was much quieter. The road to Toowoomba was one I knew well, and I expected heavy truck traffic. I would have camped near the town if I could have found a quiet place, but it was too bustling, and the surrounding areas were just vast expanses of agricultural land with no semblance of a caravan park or camping area.

Putting on my glasses, helmet, and gloves, I fired up Emu and took a deep breath, preparing for one of the most hazardous rides so far as I was growing tired. The sun was low on the horizon, necessitating extra caution. Pulling out into traffic, I gunned the engine and slipped behind a truck. The turbulence was intense, tossing me around like a rag doll. Each time I managed to escape the backwash, another road train would overtake me, starting the cycle over.

The road from Dalby to Toowoomba was packed with trucks carrying all sorts of equipment and supplies, including road trains with cattle bound for abattoirs and large mining trucks on even larger carriers. It was the most uncomfortable ride I have had so far, a constant battle to keep Emu on the left side of the left lane. The pressure waves from the giant machines just feet away were terrifying.

Eventually, I reached the outskirts of Toowoomba. The cityscape had transformed significantly since my last visit, with massive earthworks and a complex network of roads reminiscent of a spaghetti junction. This was part of the city and range bypass project, which I had heard about but was seeing for the first time. The construction, a sprawling mesh of tar and concrete, starkly contrasted with the sorghum and wheat fields I had just passed through.

The city itself is beautiful as always, and I'm lucky to be here just before the Carnival of Flowers. I know a couple of the motels in this town so rather than hunting for a place to camp I opt for a motel. Where else but the Swagman Motel on the southern outskirts?

After unpacking, I quickly rode up to Picnic Point, a popular restaurant and park area that overlooks the Lockyer Valley. As the sun set, the blue mist from the eucalypts cast a mottled hue over the valley—a perfect moment for photography. The park was lively with people exercising and couples walking hand-in-hand, enjoying the spectacular view. The sun dipped below the horizon swiftly, leaving the valley bathed in golden and green hues. From atop the Great Dividing Range, the road steeply descends into the valley, with the main highway meandering towards Brisbane in the distance. It resembled a vast watercolour painting. Returning to my room as the sun set and securing Emu under his camo cover outside, I quickly fell asleep.

Chapter 17
Riding the Scenic Rim

The accommodation was basic but fresh and clean and it had a heater, a welcome feature since Toowoomba can be quite cold in spring. I recall it even snowing here once while I was walking to the university during my brief stint as a full-time student. I once had to thaw my car's windshield with warm water to remove overnight ice—a rare necessity in Queensland, where it seldom snows.

So when I stepped outside of my room in the morning, I was greeted by the cold but crisp air. If I wasn't fully awake before, the chill certainly did the trick. I swiftly reassembled my panniers and packed up. The challenge was manoeuvring Emu, my 240-kilogram adventure bike, out from its resting spot. What seemed like a good plan the previous evening proved daunting in the crisp morning air. After attempting a 180-degree turn without damaging the surrounding plants or hitting nearby walls, I finally aligned the front wheel, donned my helmet, glasses, and gloves, and fired up the engine. I accelerated up the ramp and onto the road. Looking back, I noticed a few more lights turned on in the motel as people investigated the early morning disturbance. Thankfully, I didn't have a Harley Davidson; otherwise, I might have awakened even more neighbours. At only five in the morning, I realised it was indeed too early for such noise.

Toowoomba is one of the most liveable and beautiful cities in Queensland. I lived here for six years and completed several degrees at the University of Southern Queensland. It is one of the few places in Queensland that has all four seasons--cold and wet winters, hot summers, and changeable weather during autumn and spring. It's springtime when the city comes alive with flowers, there's even a carnival to celebrate spring. The Carnival of Flowers happens in the second week of September every year.

The town has many gardens, including the Chinese Gardens at the University of Southern Queensland, but the most spectacular is the council-managed Queens Park. There is also the most amazing flower competition with prizes for the best gardens under several different categories. The town comes alive with flowers during September. I was there at the perfect time.

The town is a gardener's dream. It is well worth spending a few days looking around Toowoomba, especially during the lead-up to the Carnival of Flowers. During winter it gets "Fucking Cold" (this is not a swear word, it's an official rating). See my temperature rating in the section about Surat. Toowoomba is an amazing place to visit at any time of the year with a vibrant pub scene and jazz at the local coffee shops. The difference between Toowoomba and the Gold Coast is like night and day. Not only the weather but the people seem to be friendlier in Toowoomba.

Today, I will ride down the Toowoomba range, then take as many country roads as I can through the Lockyer Valley to Beaudesert. Once I get to Beaudesert I will ride through Canungra and over

Mount Tamborine to Oxenford. I will then make my way to the Gold Coast Holiday Park in Helensvale. There, I will catch up with two of my long-term friends, Dave and Mandy.

It must have been a Sunday morning because opposite the Botanical Gardens in Queens Park is a market, where stall holders were busy preparing their stalls.

The sun was just poking its head over the ridge line, and the sky was clear. It was bitterly cold so I was wrapped in my down jacket with my riding jacket over the top. I walked through the park and was almost run over by park runners. I've never come across park runners before, usually, the only people out at this time are mad motorcycle riders. I was still looking for that coffee when a walker (who had a running infliction, much like myself) almost walked over me. For fuck's sake, when was a group running in a park a thing? It appears that park running is a thing and I wasn't having another one of those strange nightmares. As I pinched myself to make sure I was awake, another runner ran by, almost running over me, again. People get up early, like two in the morning, put on their gym clothes and makeup, then meet up with other insane people in the early morning to get hot and sweaty. Now, I'm not too old to appreciate getting hot and sweaty in the morning, but in this context not only don't I understand but I can't appreciate the effort they put into it. After all, not one of them looked in any way sexy, in their fitness clothing and blue-pigmented skin, clearly suffering from the cold. It occurred to me that the sexy ones were probably still in bed getting hot and sweaty in other ways.

I'm keen to get back on the road and explore the Lockyer Valley, so I decide to wait until I get to the bottom of the notorious Toowoomba Range Crossing before refuelling. The range crossing is a steep winding road and the main arterial route from the Darling Downs to Brisbane. There are trucks of all types linking the rich agricultural plains with the congested Brisbane urban sprawl and the Brisbane Port. As I rode over the crest of the Great Dividing Range, two huge road trains were blocking the dual carriageway, and a giant cattle truck was being overtaken by a 50-metre-long fuel tanker. I sat back waiting for my chance to get around the slower cattle truck. Eventually, I had enough room to manoeuvre and I was able to pass. On the side of the road, spaced at the steepest sections of the incline are long sand access tracks, these act as barriers if a truck loses its brakes on the descent, the truck driver would aim for one of the access tracks and hopefully the deep sand would be enough to stop the truck.

I remember a serious accident that held up traffic on the range for almost a day. It was tragic, a road train carrying cattle to the abattoir rolled, coming around on a tight corner. Cattle flew out of the top deck of the truck and landed on vehicles coming up the range, crushing cars, and killing their inhabitants. At least two people were killed, more were injured and over 30 head of cattle had to be shot on the road to put them out of their misery.

The bypass coming into town was meant to reduce traffic on this steep section of highway and make it safer, but it still seemed busy to me. I'm conscious of the congestion as I lean into the corners, but I drift along, slowly making sure I keep my distance and stay out of the blind spots of other drivers. Eventually, I made it safely to the bottom.

My first stop is Helidon, a thriving community of just over 1,000 people. Despite its small size, it has a fascinating history. Over 15 years ago, an infamous cult operated here, sparking controversy with rumours of strange sexual practices. Though I'm convinced these were just rumours, the cult made headlines for all the wrong reasons, with allegations of typical guru sexual misconduct, impregnations of followers, imprisonment, and forced adherence to strict religious doctrine. However, these incidents don't define this remarkable town, which was originally established in 1841 as a pastoral holding. It later became renowned for the "Oogar Dang Water," subsequently renamed Helidon Soda Water. In 1926, a health spa that utilised these waters was opened, still operational today. The local Aboriginal peoples have bathed in these waters for thousands of years, believing in their healing properties.

The road out of Helidon is a four-lane, dual carriageway that takes a direct route through acres of small crop farms, including potatoes and corn fields. The road is almost straight to Brisbane and at around 106 kilometres it is the most direct route to Queensland's capital. For a biker to get to the Gold Coast via this route you have to brave an equally dangerous and potentially suicidal five-lane M1 Highway. I would rather take the road less travelled and head through the middle of the greater Brisbane agricultural centre of the Lockyer Valley. I still haven't had my share of country roads and riding the back roads appeals to me. The valley between the Great Dividing Range and the hinterland of the Gold Coast is known as the Gold Coast Scenic Rim.

My plan is to ride towards the Cunningham Highway across the Lockyer Valley, cross the highway, and make my way to Beaudesert. I will then ride to Canungra (home of the famous tropical warfare army training centre), a town that has become synonymous with bikers as the place to meet on a Sunday morning. I then ride over Mount Tamborine to Oxenford and Helensvale, where I will catch up with my long-time mate Dave.

I couldn't help but think that bikers in this region have some of the best riding trails I've seen so far. While mostly paved, they offer great riding experiences. It's easy to imagine a Sunday morning ride from Brisbane through the valley, stopping for lunch at one of the many pubs or exploring the various Sunday markets scattered throughout the area. Although adventure bikes and Harley-Davidsons are suitable, a well-set-up cafe racer would be ideal, particularly for enjoying the twisties and long flats.

Along this journey, I discovered some great places I would like to come back to and explore over a few lazy weekends. One of these was the amazing "Lillybrook Camping Area." I was looking for a rest area to set up my camp stove and came across this little gem of a campground.

After morning coffee, I continued my ride towards the Cunningham Highway. The roads undulated through acres of grassland, and occasionally I crossed small creeks, their bridges rattling as I roared over them. The day was perfect, neither too hot nor too cold, and the scenery painted a picturesque rural landscape. After ascending a particularly steep incline, I spotted a lookout sign pointing to a concealed entryway. I ventured up the steep access road and discovered Cunningham Lookout, offering a panoramic view of the Great Dividing Range from Cunningham's Gap to the Toowoomba Range.

After checking the map, I hit the road again, dropping down the rather steep up-jump and finding myself again on a country road heading south towards the Cunningham Highway. The scenery is stunningly rural and it's difficult to sometimes remember that I'm not far from the two most congested cities in Queensland,

I'm less than 45 minutes from Mount Tamborine (above the Gold Coast) and about the same to Brisbane.

The road is slightly bumpy with some filled-in potholes making for a less-than-ideal surface, but as I ride my mind is less on the road than the many rural homesteads that scream yesteryear. These buildings are your typical Queenslanders with large sweeping verandas and high ceilings. Built to withstand the summer heat of an Australian summer and the cold of winter. Modern architects should take a lesson from these simple yet effective designs.

The Cunningham Highway is a main trucking route from Brisbane to the southern outback and on into the state of New South Wales. I cross the road and eventually find a small country track that takes me to the town of Beaudesert. I lament on what a great road this would be if I was on a sports bike or a cafe racer, the tight clear corners leading to the left then straightening up ready for the right-hander. I make a mental note if I ever got such a bike I would come down here to ride these amazing roads. It's not long before the typical signage that heralds my arrival in another town starts to appear on billboards. This time it is the town of Beaudesert. Beaudesert is a surprisingly big country town with significant facilities and community. I have an image of a single service station and hopefully a bakery, but it is far more than that. There are all sorts of facilities available, including a bakery, where I stop for a quick toasted sandwich and milk coffee. While sitting at an outside table, I watch groups of bikes heading up towards Canungra.

Following a couple of Harley riders, I set off for Canungra, as I get closer the traffic starts to get heavier. There are craft shops, cafes, pubs, and all sorts of tourist attractions. Long gone are those days when I used to come over from Oxenford to the Canungra hotel for a laidback country blues band and a few Bourbon and Cokes. While I would have loved to stop to reminisce about old times when life was slower, now's not that time. It's getting late and the sun is starting to go down behind me. I'm catching up with my mate Dave and spending a couple of days with him and his wife at the Gold Coast Holiday Park in Helensvale.

The road to Mount Tamborine is an absolute biker paradise, with long straight sections ending in sweeping cambered corners and then twisty hills climbs. Once you've done that, it's just "set and repeat" six or seven more times. I was having so much fun I almost missed the turnoff for Mount Tamborine.

The ride up to Mount Tamborine is a very steep hill climb and another awesome biker road. There are a couple of ways up the range, and any of the roads is an adventure in their own right. I took the steep and infamous Henry Roberts Drive. It twists and turns and climbs incredibly steeply. But once on top, there's stunning scenery and magnificent views out through the Lockyer Valley to the Great Diving Range. You pretty much ride the ridge line with a few ups and downs. Along the way, there are all sorts of pubs, accommodation houses, and of course, the craft and tourist strips. I ride through a place called the "Eagles Nest" with its craft shops and art galleries. It's not long and I'm descending to Oxenford.

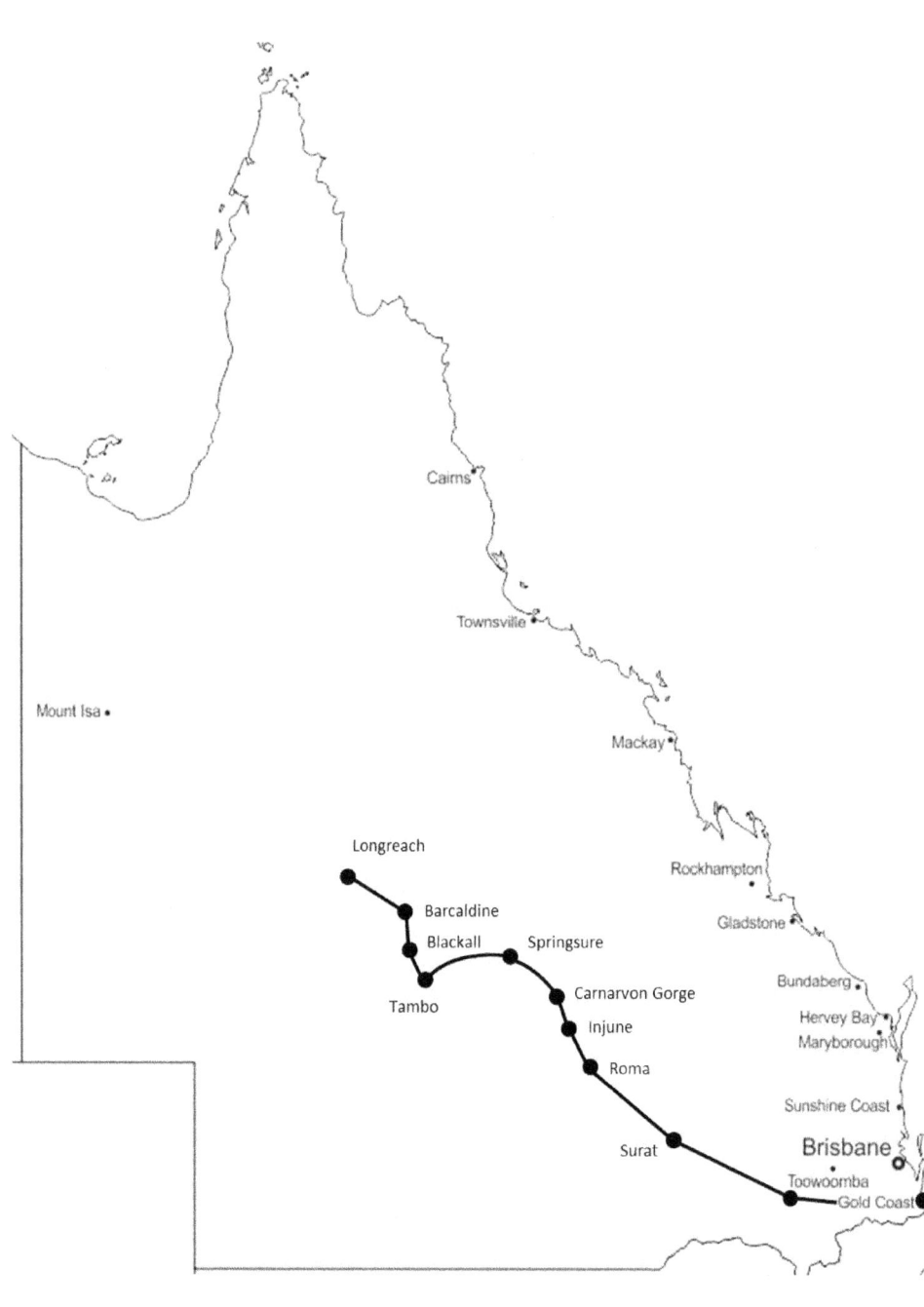

Emu and I at the Barcoo River Rest Area - Blackall

Monument to the poor dead tree of knowledge and the Labor Party - Barcaldine

The border of civilisation, Black Stump - Blackall

Tambo Teddy Bears, home of the Teddy Bears Picnic - Tambo

Chicken Racing at "The Royal Carrangarra Hotel", Tambo

Intersection of the Wilderness Way and the Dawson Development Road-Springsure

A1 Used Cars, Cobb and Co Way - Southwest Queensland

Stealth camping on a cliff somewhere near Springsure – Central Queensland

Emus first creek crossing, Carnarvon Gorge – Central Queensland

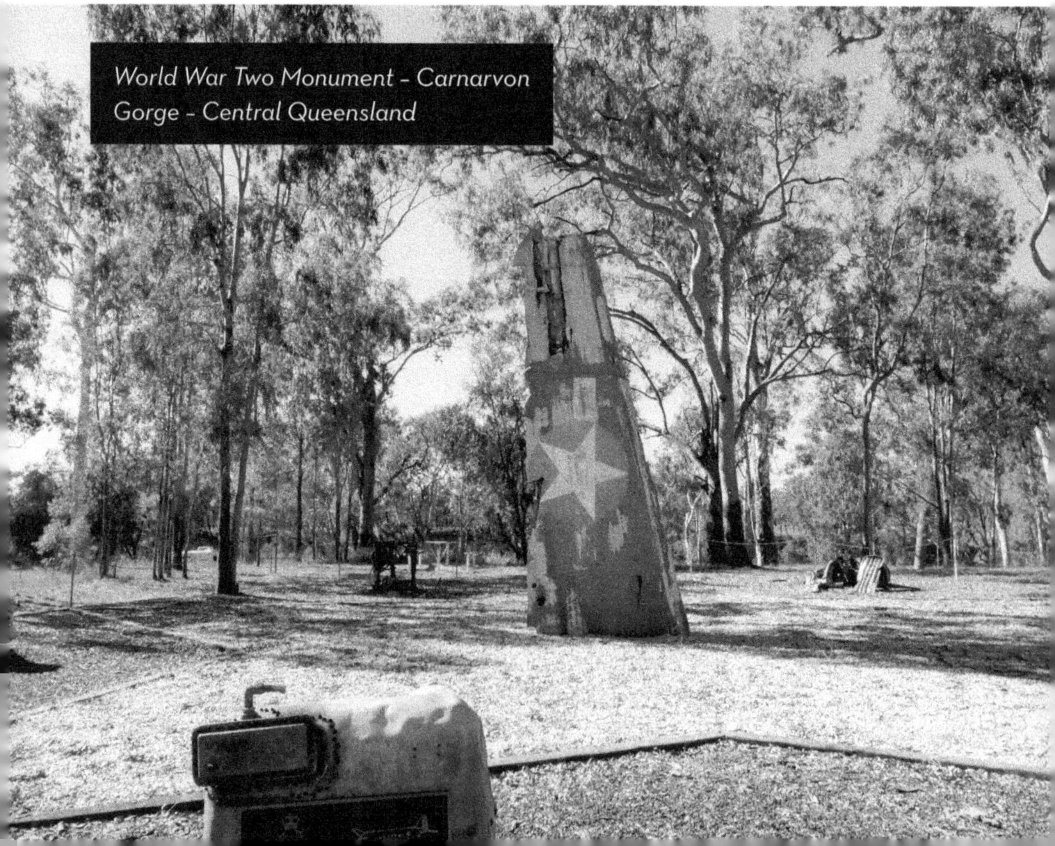

World War Two Monument – Carnarvon Gorge – Central Queensland

Free camping at Fisherman's Park - Surrat

Cenotaph in the botanical garden during the Carnival of Flowers - Toowoomba

Cunninghams Lookout, Scenic Rim - Southeast Queensland

Gold Coast Holiday Park, sanctuary from the hustle and bustle of the Gold Coast - Southeast Queensland

Coolangatta, coffee with infinite possibilities – Gold Coast

World famous surf beach – Kirra Beach, Gold Coast

Chapter 18
From Rustic to Rush Hour - the Gold Coast Experience

"A car's weakest part is the nut holding the steering wheel"

— Unknown

I've been riding along dirt tracks, country roads, and rural highways. My journey today ends when I arrive at Helensvale on the Gold Coast. I'm staying the night with a good mate of mine and his wife at the Gold Coast Holiday Park in Helensvale.

The short journey over Mount Tamborine to the Gold Coast is like stepping from a rustic environment to that of a world of continuous rush hour traffic. I get the sense that I've entered a plastic-apocalyptic future. It all starts with traffic: you either put up with it or you do your best to avoid it. I hate traffic, especially cars and trucks when I'm on a motorcycle. I would be more accepting of cars on my roads if they were a little bit more respectful, but when you know that every car on the road is trying to kill you, it's slightly disconcerting.

Riding through the small rural town of Oxenford does nothing to prepare me for the chaotic M1 Motorway. I ride down the onramp in front of me are five lanes of traffic, I speed up to 110 kilometres per hour, but I'm still not fast enough to merge into the constant stream of cars, trucks, and vans. I twist the throttle, and Emu starts to whine; it's faster than I have ever ridden him. He's now sitting close to 6,000 rpm and clocking almost 130 kph. I finally slip into traffic and quickly make for the slow lane.

Despite being in what's officially the slow lane, at 110 kilometers per hour, it doesn't stop some drivers from tailgating. One car gets so close that I can't even see its number plate in my mirror. The driver zooms past, then cuts in front with less than a meter to spare.

It's interesting how a car seems to give people freedom, security, and superiority. What would happen if she got stopped at the red light and a big six-foot-two biker took exception to her behaviour and decided to take out his frustrations on her car? As it turns out, she has to stop at the red lights and the resulting traffic jams. So, I filter through the traffic beep my horn and wave at her as I ride past. Not today, but it brings back memories of my stapler fixation and I chose not to let her ruin my day.

Gone are the friendly waves to passing motorists and the casual nods to fellow bikers indicating, "I see you, brother/sister, safe journey." Yep, I'm on my way to a new country, one that doesn't follow the same road rules as the one I just left. It's called Southeast Queensland.

Wow, what a fucking intense adrenaline rush—two kilometres of sheer terror—and then I turn off at the sign that says "Gold Coast Holiday Park." I pull over at the entrance and give my mate Dave a call. "I'm here, mate… I've got a bottle of red wine, let me in. There are a whole lot of fucking aliens out here driving cars, trying to kill me."

Dave and his wife Mandy and I go way back, almost 30 years to when I lived on the Gold Coast. Dave and I spent many lazy Sundays at Fisherman's Wharf. I was in my twenties, and it was a place ripe with opportunity. I watched the area grow until eventually, it began to choke with traffic. At that point, I left to study communications and journalism in Toowoomba. I've only been back twice in the past 20 years. Back then, I hatched a plan to ride a motorcycle around Australia—it was going to be on an F650 BMW—but I went to university and, as they say, the rest is history. So, in a way, I'm returning to where this dream started.

It seems my outback adventure has come to an end. I've been on the road now for about 12 days and I've travelled through some of Australia's most iconic historical landmarks and read about some of the defining events in Australia's short history. I'm now at the bottom of the State of Queensland on the Gold Coast, one of the most famous beachside regions in Australia.

The first time I arrived on the Gold Coast, it was the winter of 1986. I stayed with a friend in her small apartment just off the main highway. It was a 1960s-style unit block at the southern entrance to Surfers Paradise. Out the front was a fastfood outlet called "Chickery Chick." It reminded me of those road movies you see on Route 66 in America, with the flashing neon lights casting coloured shadows on the walls.

Having lived in eastern Melbourne, I wasn't used to the sound of the sea. I woke at four in the morning, alert and ready to embrace an adventure. Silently, I left the unit and walked the two blocks to the beach. I was the only person there, sitting in the soft sand, mesmerised by the gently rolling surf. I could taste the saltiness in the air and felt content as the gentle warm sea breeze brushed through my hair. The blue skies, moderate temperature, and gentle sea breeze were paradise to me—a stark contrast to my life as a tradesperson in a cold grey factory in Noble Park. It seemed there were endless possibilities in this exciting entrepreneurial landscape.

Within an hour, the sun peeked over the horizon, turning the ocean pink and orange. If there was a rainbow serpent, it was here on this day. Within minutes of the sunrise, another person appeared, followed by another, until there was a line of people walking just above the tidal mark, each in the other's footsteps. It's strange how moments in your life stay with you through the ages. If I close my eyes, I can see myself sitting on the beach, feel the sand between my toes, and taste the salty air.

Dave, Mandy, and I reminisced through the night over too many bottles of red wine. Eventually, I managed to sleep, waking early the next morning. After making myself a cup of coffee—Dave and Mandy still asleep in the main bedroom—I took my cup outside near the resort's swimming pool. The water was still and calm, undisturbed by noisy children. The sounds of early morning traffic filtered through as some motorists tried to beat the rush. When Dave joined me, we ordered eggs benedict and large café lattes for breakfast and sat discussing the significant changes on the Gold Coast, particularly the increasing congestion. Soon, I would have to join the throng of vehicles heading south, taking my life into my hands once more.

The border of Queensland starts at the Tweed River and stretches north to the tip of Cape York. Beyond that are the islands of the Torres Strait. In that moment, I realised my journey needed to extend to the tip. A new bucket list item was forming in my mind: traveling to Cape York, a stark contrast to the glitzy part of Queensland where I currently was. The details were still vague, but the idea was taking shape. Dave noticed my preoccupation. "You seem deep in thought," he said. "What's on your mind?" "Just figuring out how to ride to Cape York," I replied. "It's a long way, mate," he said. "Yep," I replied, "I'd better get started."

After hugging Mandy and shaking Dave's hand with a "See ya next time, mate," I mounted my bike. It almost felt like I was a cowboy swinging onto a horse, ready to ride off into the sunset. Instead, I pressed the starter, and the deep, throaty sound of the big 650 came to life, echoing off the resort buildings. This felt right; I was doing something not many others do. Dressed in black Kevlar jeans, dusty adventure boots, a heavy adventure jacket, and a black helmet, I looked—and for the first time, truly felt—like a biker.

It's an interesting feeling when you see your self-image changing. I have now started to align myself to a way of life that is completely different from the one I started this journey in. I'm now aligning my thinking with the biker culture and to that of an adventurer. I wonder what that means? Culture is one of those things that everybody talks about but many find it hard to grasp, like trying to grasp sunlight in your hands. It can be defined as the customs, traditions, values, beliefs, language, and practices that a group of people share. Up until this point in my life, my culture has been the customs, values, and beliefs of the middle-class professional worker. I wasn't always that, either: in my early life, I was a broke factory worker, then an apprentice, tradesperson, and eventually a Director of a TAFE College. Each of these stages required a shift in thinking about who I was, this shift took years and now as I ride slowly out of the caravan park, I can see myself changing once again.

No longer do I see myself as just another commuter on the Gold Coast Highway, bracing for the inevitable traffic jam. Stepping outside my previous cultural habits has revealed them as a form of social control. Viewing life from this new angle is intriguing, reminiscent of the scene in *The Matrix* where Morpheus offers Neo the choice between the red pill and the blue pill. I chose the red pill, and everything changed.

I'm now heading south down an access road, beside me on a raised concrete platform is the Gold Coast Highway. I can hear cars whizzing past, at high speeds. I'm a little nervous about joining this rat race, but I know I have to grin and bear it; it's the only way south.

As I reach the on-ramp, I start to accelerate. I'm now doing 120 kph and well over 5,000 revs per minute. Looking for a gap to pull into, I'm twisting and stretching my head around while at the same time trying to ensure the car in front of me doesn't brake hard. Suddenly, a car changes lanes, creating the perfect opening for me. I merge, then adjust my speed to increase my following distance, measuring it by silently counting "1and, 2and, 3and" to ensure it's adequate.

Soon, I reach Nerang, a small town on the outskirts of the Great Dividing Range. Memories flood back from the time I lived here, the faces of old acquaintances flickering through my mind like scenes from an old movie. The highway, now tripled in size with wide concrete barriers, makes the town barely recognisable. The sun is already high, and the heat from the tar and concrete intensifies under the unyielding sun. The barriers block any breeze, making it the most uncomfortable ride yet. I continue toward the border and the town of Coolangatta, contemplating the changes around me.

One noticeable aspect of the Gold Coast Highway is the heavy traffic. It detracts from the scenic drive, especially when you're trying to take the kids to the beach on a hot day, and they're ratty. The struggle often involves circling around in search of a non-existent parking spot. Alternatively, you might end up parking 10 minutes away and then have to carry an inflatable duck while holding your children's hands. Yes, I hear you say, that sounds like fun. This scenario almost epitomises the typical tourist experience on the Gold Coast. The best strategy would be to book a beachfront unit and limit your travels.

The M1 connects with the Hume Highway in Brisbane and transitions into the Gold Coast Highway before becoming the Hume Highway again at the border. My journey continues to Tugun, a short ride from the beach. The highway is lined with surf shops, juice bars, beauty salons, and a plethora of fast food outlets, which gradually give way to towering accommodation blocks. To my right is the Gold Coast Airport.

I change lanes and veer left, passing the impressive beachside headquarters of the famous "Billabong" clothing brand. Soon, I'm riding past Kirra Point, known for its iconic surf breaks—a paradise for surfers. I arrive in Coolangatta, at the renowned Coolangatta Hotel, a hotspot for star-studded parties in the 80s and 90s, some of which I was fortunate to attend.

Coolangatta is famous for being the first place in Australia to run an Ironman competition—a grueling swim, surf ski, and run event known as the Coolangatta Gold. Today, Ironman contests are held throughout the summer across Australia. Coolangatta is also celebrated as the filming location for the quintessentially Australian film, *Muriel's Wedding*.

Coolangatta and Tweed Heads comprise the Twin Towns, divided by the state border. In the 70s, 80s, and 90s, slot machines were illegal in Queensland but not in New South Wales. Large clubs sprung up in Tweed Heads, offering subsidised meals, free live entertainment, and slot machines—known locally as "pokies." Gold Coast residents would flock to these clubs for a night out, creating a mini Las Vegas. Many believed slot machines remained illegal in Queensland primarily because they diverted revenue from the illegal casinos operating in Surfers Paradise.

The beaches start on the northern side of the Tweed River, with famous names such as Snapper Rocks, Duranba, and Greenmount, which are well known to surfers as some of the best point breaks in the world. I ride down the beach esplanade and find a coffee shop; it's trendy and the people here look like wannabe fashion models. I order my cafe latte and I'm asked what sort of milk I want, there's about 10 choices from low-fat to coconut to soy. "No thanks, just cow's milk," and then I'm asked if I want a decaffeinated, double shot, full shot, half shot quarter shot, or some other unknown variation. "No, just one shot, thanks." Then I'm asked if I would like Kenyan, Morrocan, or Columbian. "No, just coffee, please." Fuck sake, I could have made it myself at the park and saved 10 bucks and all this aggravation. I'm sitting on a small veranda, Emu is parked just below me, I wonder if it would be rude to just get my stove out and boil some water and make my full-strength instant coffee with full cream milk. But then my latte arrives and all is forgiven.

In front of me is the esplanade road and parkland in front of Coolangatta Beach, It's a beautiful winter's morning and there are perfectly formed waves coming around Greenmount

Point. Coolangatta Beach would be one of the Gold Coast's best beaches and perfect for family fun. Coolangatta itself is a shopping paradise, especially if you're into surfwear or surfing in general. It's where the next stage of my adventure up the coast of Queensland begins.

When I was 22, I bought a caravan and lived at the Tweed River Banora Point Caravan Park. I was into sailboarding so I used to sail up and down the river. It's at this time in my life that I took up SCUBA diving, when it was calm and difficult to sail I would jump into the river at the bar wall and snorkel along it until the tide changed and the current became too hard to swim against. I didn't care too much about sharks, but the river is known for bull sharks, but I only saw one the whole time I dived there. I have also seen eagle rays, dolphins, octopuses and all manner of fish in that small but wonderful ecosystem. Just off the coast on the Tweed side is a small island known as Hook Island, it's where I learnt to SCUBA dive, I've seen whales breach nearby and hundreds of stingrays feed on the sea grass on the western side of the island.

Once I've finished my Columbian latte with cow's milk and natural brown sugar from Queensland, I make my way to the beach to take some photos for my blog and then I'm back on the road. This time just north of Coolangatta is the famous and incredibly impressive point break called Kirra Point. When the swells are rolling in this place is sheer heaven for those that can handle big surf. The point creates the perfect barrel and many a star surfer has adorned the pages of surfing magazines riding through the ultimate tube at this point. It's often home to the national surfing championships and rivals Bells Beach in the famous surfing locations stakes.

Kirra Point is such a famous surfing spot that surf riders have built a pavilion just for watching the surfing action. It's on the main footpath and extends over the rocks at the southern end of the road. I take my time getting just the right photo. Unfortunately, today is not a good surf day as the sea is almost glassed out.

In no time, I'm back on the road heading north. The strip of "golden sand" that constitutes most of the Gold Coast beaches starts at Coolangatta and finishes at the mouth of the Nerang River. The beach has several unique places where people tend to gather, most around the headlands where there is a good point break or protected inlets. I will concentrate on those parts rather than every little sign posted beach.

Travelling through these places is like travelling back in time for me through my memories. I used to drive this road in an old 1977 HX Holden Kingswood with salt in my hair, exhausted from SCUBA diving at Hook Island and looking forward to catching up with mates at Fisherman's Wharf. What could have been, had I stayed on the Gold Coast? I'd put on my favourite cassette and "Dock of the Bay" would be playing. Did I make the right decision to leave and attend university in Toowoomba? What would my life have been like if I had made other decisions? This adventure I'm on is not just about testing my resilience; it's about examining why I am where I am. Although it's becoming clearer that where I am in my life now is a result of the actions I took or opportunities I didn't take, I'm not sure looking back is the best way to move forward. It becomes clear that any decision can have an infinite number of possible outcomes, including the decision to do nothing. This is the essence of karma; I'm beginning to think the way forward is to build a pathway of opportunities and rely on karma to make it all work out in the end. It's also becoming clear that looking backwards only reinforces older ways of thinking.

I'm pulled back from my metacognitive ramblings by the number of cars that have just joined the Gold Coast Highway. I'm climbing over the Currumbin Escarpment, and soon I'll be able to see Currumbin Alley. I've just past the old Currumbin Wildlife Sanctuary, still operating and vibrant after all these years. The small Currumbin Creek that meanders through the valley opens up into a small but deep estuary before flowing out the mouth to the sea. This is affectionately known as Currumbin Alley. I take a left at the access way and wind down under the giant bridge that spans the alley, then I ride along the southern side of the estuary before rounding the point and coming face to face with the Currumbin Rock and surf life-saving club precariously perched on a giant rock on the beach.

Currumbin Rock has been made famous by TV presentations on ANZAC day doing live crosses of the proceedings with the rock in the background. It makes for a majestic backdrop as the sun comes up and the waves crash over the rock. The surf club sits at the base of the rock and is often affected by the tidal surge. You can climb the rock to a lookout and observe the beautiful sandy strip. As a beach, though it has some disadvantages, being perched on a rock escarpment it becomes more susceptible to tidal movements and therefore rips and sweeps, which can be dangerous to swimmers.

After taking more photos for my blog, I ride back to the Alley. As a young man, I learnt to sailboard here. During low tide or as the tide turns during the high tide mark the alley is remarkably calm and an awesome place to learn to surf or swim. However, at the extreme of both tidal phases, the alley can be dangerous due to the large volume of water being drawn out the Currumbin Creek and the relatively small mouth of the river.

Having spent time walking on the beach and dipping my toes in the salty waters of the Gold Coast, it was time to move on. Riding up the Gold Coast Highway, I travel through Palm Beach and then straight on to the next headland. It's the middle of the day and the heat is tortuous in riding gear and body armour. I come to a small parkland on the left with a creek and another small estuary. This is Tullebudgera Creek, another place for popular young families. There used to be a famous nightclub just next to this park called the Play Room, it was a great hangout for surfers in particular, but anybody was welcome. It wasn't just a nightclub but an institution and you could hear live music any night of the week. It was a place for many of Australia's best bands. It had a playlist of the very best, including Little River Band, Cold Chisel, Jimmy and the Boys, Midnight Oil, The Angles, MiSex, Split Enz, and even the legendary INXS played there. There was a vibe about the Gold Coast back in the 1970s and 80s that has since been replaced by concrete and plastic. I guess to some extent it mirrors the change in society. On the left side of the highway used to be a big family caravan park. Today, it's a tourist park, but still has some camping facilities by the water.

I continue over the headland and ride down into Burleigh Heads, known to the locals as one of the best beachside suburbs of the Gold Coast and like Coolangatta has a giant point break.

Burleigh Heads is about halfway along the stretch of sand from Coolangatta to Surfers Paradise. While there are many beaches in between, Burleigh is one of the most famous. It would sit alongside Coolangatta and Surfers Paradise, in terms of being in the public consciousness. Like Coolangatta, Burleigh Beach is tucked behind a small headland. This breaks the swell and causes the formation of some of the most iconic surf breaks in the country. International surf competitions are held at Burleigh Heads.

Burleigh Heads is a vibrant township with a number of really good restaurants and coffee houses, not to mention other facilities such as the famous bowels club right next to the highway. There is plenty of parking near the town and lots of shady trees.

Burleigh Heads lacks the flashy tourist hype of Surfers Paradise, but it compensates with easier accessibility. I found parking here easier than anywhere else. As the afternoon began to fade, I was preparing to stay with my niece and her boyfriend in a town called Ashmore. However, I had one last stop to make: Surfers Paradise. I have mentioned this place earlier in my story. While I am not a fan of its glitz and artificiality, no guide to Queensland's beaches would be complete without a mention of Surfers Paradise. The beach here is part of the continuous stretch of long golden sands that begin at Burleigh Heads and extend through to Main Beach and the Gold Coast Spit.

The allure of a beach life, mingled with opportunity and sophistication, is too much for some people; many have migrated north to enjoy the ultimate sea change. Often, they drift back over time, disenchanted at the dog-eat-dog culture of the strip.

If you look at Surfers Paradise as a beach, you may be slightly disappointed. While it is part of the long and seemingly never-ending golden sandy ribbon from Coolangatta through to the Spit at Main Beach, the Surfers Paradise beach itself is only one small part of that golden ribbon.

It is a section of heavily manicured sand, with sand grooming machinery ploughing the beach each morning. The Gold Coast

Councils spend millions of dollars each year cultivating the image that is "Surfers Paradise."

Surfers Paradise Beach has largely remained the same, while high-rises and shops have come and gone. In the '80s and '90s, the entrepreneurs were dubbed the "White Shoe Brigade," as white shoes were in vogue—I even had a pair myself! Each year, thousands of beach-loving tourists flock to this golden strip to soak up the endless Queensland sun. They often end up purchasing overpriced clothing, fridge magnets, beach towels, and T-shirts emblazoned with "Two states to be in, Pissed and Queensland," along with numerous plastic souvenirs.

Having revisited my history with this place, I'm starting to feel tired. Tonight, I plan to catch up with my niece, her boyfriend, and their dog Alana in Ashmore—if only I could find my way there. One aspect of the Gold Coast that always intrigued me was the rapid construction of high-rise buildings. Now, without my usual landmarks, I find myself riding in circles. This loss of familiar navigation points, compounded by newly developed roads, is causing me considerable distress. After several backtracks, I eventually locate Ashmore, but it still takes about an hour to find their address. I've resolved to buy a GPS before continuing much further on my adventure.

Chapter 19
Cafe Racing

"Riding a motorcycle on today's highways, you have to ride in a very defensive manner. You have to be a good rider and you have to have both hands and both feet on the controls at all times."

— Evel Knievel

The term Cafe Racing is not very often discussed in my adventure riding groups. I like the concept but I guess it is a term best used in cities, rather than rural adventure riding. It had its foundation in 1950s post-war England, where motorcycles were the only form of transport available to the youth. They used to race from cafe to cafe on modified bikes. My father was one of these bikers. He was a member of the ton-up club and once held a racing record from London to Brighton. This was in the days when the TT Isle of Man was in its infancy and rockers and mods were at war with each other. It conjures images of leather jackets, Elvis Presley and Johnny Cash, fighting off the inroads of the Beatles and Rolling Stones.

During this section of my ride, I come face to face with modern cafe racing. I have to admit leaning into corners and powering out onto long wide flats appeals to my boy racer inner child, but it has been buried deep down. Unfortunately, I'm not sure if Emu is up to the challenge.

It's a new day and I'm getting myself prepared for riding up the treacherous M1 Freeway to Brisbane. Although if I can help it, I will try and go around the city and avoid the toll roads. As I ride down the on-ramp from Nerang to the Gaven Way, I see a wall of cars; I can't help feeling that a bike with a bit of racing spirit wouldn't be a bad thing about now.

The traffic seems to have closed up as I get closer. I have two choices: stop or speed up while pretending to slow down. I drop down a gear, then when the driver sees that I'm trying to get in behind her, she slows down. Just then I accelerate and find the gap in front. I can tell she's pissed at me, and for the next five kilometres, she stays about two metres off my arse. Either she likes my arse or she's just being a bitch, I'm not sure how I feel about either of those conclusions.

I'm conscious of staying out of the blind spot of the motorist in front of me while looking back to see where the zombie driver from hell is. I look across, hoping the driver next to me will show some acknowledgement that I'm there at least. To my surprise, all I see is a blank, emotionless face.

Looking further across the five lanes of traffic, I see more grey-faced motorists. It's like I've entered some sort of zombie apocalypse—the more I look the more I see. I'm thinking to myself, damn, just as well I packed for this very occurrence. But unfortunately, I left the zombie-killing gear at my parents-in-law's place as part of the equipment culling I went through to reduce weight. Now I'm regretting that decision.

It's like a brigade of depressed motor car drivers heading to work after a weekend of trying to find car parks at the beach.

I'm a little concerned at what I have just seen, what hope is there for a lonely motorcyclist to be seen, and I'm determined to ride my race. I accelerate into the gap, then change lanes, then accelerate again until I'm clear of traffic; well, as clear as I can be. This darting in and out of traffic is typical of being a cafe racer and I wonder about the feasibility of buying one for myself.

Robert Pirsig in his book, *Zen and the Art of Motorcycle Maintenance*, wrote of a similar experience:

"It was all those people in the cars coming the other way," she says. "The first one looked so sad. And then the next one looked exactly the same way, and then the next one and the next one, they were all the same."

Pirsig's observations resonate deeply with me. It appears that momentarily stepping away from the rat race provides fresh insights into a different kind of life—one that we mistakenly accept as normal due to societal conditioning. In this life, we often surrender our autonomy to corporations or false idols, believing it to be normal until the pressure becomes unbearable. Sometimes, this pressure erupts disastrously, and a hapless manager might end up with a stapler lodged in his arse, while the perpetrator faces Human Resources for breaching a vaguely defined Code of Conduct. Having been in senior management for over 20 years, I've yet to encounter a Code of Conduct that explicitly forbids stapler misuse, even if it's deserved.

Pirsig's words have lingered in my mind since I first read his book over 20 years ago. It's time for a reread. Pirsig discusses the concept of "quality" as a means to balance romantic and classical values—essential for maintaining sanity. This balance is akin to what we experience when riding motorcycles and embarking on adventures. The classical aspects involve planning, preparation, and maintenance of our bikes and ourselves, while the romantic aspects are about the journey, achievements, and the stories we share.

Today, I'm riding about 250 kilometres to the Sunshine Coast, aiming to bypass Brisbane and its chaotic traffic, as well as avoid toll fees. Despite having a poor map and limited experience dodging Brisbane, I managed to find a route that skirted the city centre. It took me about two hours, but I successfully avoided tolls. I'm still not close to the Sunshine Coast, but I've reached a northern suburb called "The Gap."

The Gap is a serene, forested suburb, ideal for a lunch break in a secluded park, just two and a half hours from the Gold Coast. Lunch consisted of coffee, a tuna and pasta packet, and a couple of muesli bars, enjoyed under the shade of trees. I considered camping here for the night with just a small bike swag for cover, but I decided against it since I had sent my hammock home as part of reducing my gear.

The Gap serves as a gateway from the greater Brisbane urban area. I found a small track on the map that seemed to wind around the major highways, potentially leading me towards the upper Maroochydore River.

I remember reading about a route in a motorcycle book that covered Mount Glorious and then continued along the range to Mount Nebo. Described as an unofficial racing circuit, I wasn't sure if Emu or my riding gear was suitable for the journey. Nonetheless, a sign just outside The Gap pointed towards Mount Glorious. As I was on a motorcycle adventure, it would have been remiss of me not to find out what all l the fuss was about. The journey began just after leaving The Gap, winding through the

Samford Valley—an incredible ride through farmland and sub-tropical forests.

My weight distribution on the bike is much better than it had been and I find myself more connected to Emu. The road is only a secondary road so it's relatively narrow and bumpy, but I'm enjoying the wallowing corners and long straights. It occurred to me that this was another biker's paradise, then I heard the unmistakable roar of high-revving sports bikes. I got a glimpse of what looked like a green Kawasaki Ninja 1000 and a red Honda CBR750, as they zipped past me like missiles, their engines screaming.

I had inadvertently found myself on someone's personal racetrack. I tried to keep up, but Emu wasn't cut out for café racing, and they soon vanished. At the first corner, they both leaned into the turn with knees out, reminiscent of a Grand Prix rivalry or a scene from the TT Isle of Man.

The road started to climb and twist through the sub-tropical rainforest. Emu responded beautifully to the corners; you could tell he was enjoying the opportunity to pretend to be a race bike. On a few corners, I had to drop down a gear and straighten up, or my panniers would have scraped against the ground. There was no sign of our racing friends. Before long we came to a tee intersection, Mount Nebo to the left, Mount Glorious to the right. Just as I was making my mind up a large white BMW sped past.

I only just saw a flash of the blue and red colour scheme, but it was enough for me to realise even the police like this road and while they may not stop at the cafe, they are effectively cafe racing. Better I'm behind them than the other way around, so I followed until the top of Mount Glorious came into view.

I thought if the police can race up this road, so can I. But in reality, no police officer is going to get a speeding ticket so I just let that thought die a natural death. It needs to be said that cafe racing on a KLR650 is not the same as cafe racing on a Ninja H2 or a Yamaha R1. Just so we have that clear, my tyres were dedicated off-road and definitely wouldn't handle the sort of cornering a cafe racer or sports bike would. It's not clear if the police officer stopped for a coffee at the cafe racer hangout, but it wouldn't surprise me if she came back later.

Eventually, I realised I was lost. Approaching a couple of bikers near the Mount Glorious café, I asked them, "Where am I?" Bikers are some of the friendliest people I've met, and within moments, three of them were giving me detailed directions to Woodford, my next major destination.

There was a beautiful BMW Dakar R100 GS, fully restored over by another table with a white-haired gentleman next to it. He was dressed more like me and I sat down opposite and introduced myself. We talked about bikes and adventure riding for some time and he gave me excellent directions and warned me about places the police like to hide and wait for unsuspecting bikers. Police like to stake out this area, I couldn't think why they would, sarcastically looking around at my fellow bikers in full leather racing kit, even though it was over thirty degrees Celsius. I showed him my KLR and he said it probably wouldn't be a problem for me, proving that everyone's a comedian.

I said goodbye to my new friends and headed back down the range to Samford to refuel and then onto Mount Nee, before heading towards Woodford and then the Sunshine Coast.

Did you know there's a phenomenon called fuel station rage? After filling up Emu and walking inside to pay, I returned to find a small red car had squeezed in front of my bike, reversing right up to the front wheel. Considering there were eleven other pumps available and we were the only customers, I was understandably annoyed. The driver was so close that I had to back Emu up a metre and a half just to get around the car. When I asked her why she had done that, she just gave me a smug look. I felt enraged by her attitude to common decency. While I was tempted to leave a lasting impression on her car, I took a deep breath and shook my head, pulled out, and continued towards Woodford. It's crucial on the road to not let incidents like these dictate your emotions. Why should I let this person's poor behaviour ruin my day? While my thoughts were on her behaviour they were not where they should be which was on the road and riding safely.

The road from Samford to Woodford goes through some amazing country, it's an up-and-down, twisting sort of road that steadily climbs up to Mount Nee before descending to the D'Aguila Highway. You travel through towns including Kobble Creek, Dayboro, Ocean View, Delaney Creek, and D'Aguilar before finally coming to Woodford. The road opens up at times to some of the most spectacular views of the D'Aguilar National Park and the Delaneys Creek Forest.

Woodford is a vibrant and interesting town that sits on the edge of the Glass House Mountains and bisects the D'Aguila Highway leading to Beewah. When I first drove through Woodford over 30 years ago, it was a quiet country town. Now, it has a coffee shop on each corner and at least two motorbikes out the front of each of them. Motorcycle tourism is flourishing here, making it a rider's paradise between the Gold Coast hinterland and Brisbane.

It was starting to get late in the afternoon and I was looking for a place to pull up for the night. Just outside of Woodford is Cruice Park, a free camping area. I stopped and had a look around. It has excellent facilities, but I thought I could find some stealth camping further up the road, giving me more time in the morning to explore some beaches.

You know how sometimes you have a gut feeling about things? Mine was saying pull up and camp. You should always listen to your gut feeling. Instead of stopping, I carried on; I was incredibly tired and becoming more and more irritable. By the time I got closer to the coast, I was looking for places to stop and wild camp. There are no out-of-the-way places on the Sunshine Coast that would enable me to pull up. The whole place has been built out. Finally, I got to the Sunshine Coast Highway at about six in the evening, the sun was on the horizon and I was now riding in the twilight. I made my way straight to Maroochydore and found the Cotton Tree Caravan Park.

When the young girl at the check-in asked for fifty dollars per night I almost fell over. I only wanted a non-powered campsite. I will listen to my gut feeling next time. Weaving my way through massive caravans and equally expensive four-wheel drives, I finally managed to find my site. I was pleased to see it was right on the point next to the beach.

I put Emu's camo cover on and crawled into my home away from home. Tomorrow, I would explore the beaches of the Sunshine Coast. That night, I had strange dreams of café racing and winning the TT Isle of Man.

Chapter 20
The Sunshine Coast

"How inappropriate to call the planet 'Earth' when it's clearly 'Ocean'."
— http://www.dailytravelpill.com

My campsite was at the eastern end of the caravan park in the small town of Cotton Tree, a beachside community at the end of the Maroochydore River on the Sunshine Coast. I lay in my tent listening to the surf, the sun's not quite over the horizon yet. It's time for a coffee, so I get up and find my stove, pour water into the pot, and light the burner. Within minutes, I have hot coffee steaming away in the cool breeze. I walk five metres and I'm learning on the wooden rail that separates the campsite from the beach. There's a soft glow across the horizon as the sun makes its way over the water. The inky black sky is fading to a navy blue and then purple. It's a cool morning, the small yellow ball is just peeking above the horizon and wisps of golden light are mixing with the light green sea, making for a kaleidoscope of colours. The Cotton Tree estuary is glassed out, not a breath of wind disturbs the water. There are paddle boarders out in the surf catching waves already. This is without doubt one of the Sunshine Coast's most popular beaches. I set up some shots of surfers and surf, then looked back and captured some stunning photos of the sun reflected in the windows of a number of high-rise accommodation buildings. The hills in the distance are a shadowy backdrop to the glitzy buildings in the foreground.

The feeling you get from sleeping near the beach is a luxury not afforded to many people, even though we live on an island surrounded by sea. Why is it that we so desperately want to be by the sea? I'm perplexed over this and to clarify my thoughts I decide to take a walk along the beach with my second cup of coffee. The water is warm and the sand is soft but slightly abrasive on my skin as I sink into it. It looks like the tide is coming.

I often ask myself, "What makes a perfect beach?" Is it the juxtaposition between the sand and the surf? Or perhaps the feelings we get from being near or in the water? Maybe it's the promise of relaxation offered by the beachside community?

Queensland has so much to offer the world in terms of scenery. It is well known for the Great Barrier Reef, rainforests, and surfing spots, and, of course, its beaches. When I reached Coolangatta, I set a goal to visit all the beaches in Queensland. Today, I decided to explore the southern part of the Sunshine Coast before heading to one of my favourite areas, Noosa.

The sound of traffic was jarring as I rode down the main road through Maroochydore to Mooloolaba, and then along the extensive suburban stretch to Caloundra. Although the beach runs parallel to the main road, accessing it required navigating through a high-density residential area, reminiscent of the soulless expressions of drivers I had passed on the Gold Coast.

There is an interesting contrast between the people I meet on my travels and the people I see in their cars. It's like there's a switch that turns them on and off; I guess we all have that switch.

If the switch stays off for too long, life seems to fall into a mundane sameness. Not so on a motorcycle; there's always some idiot trying to kill you so you can't afford to be "turned off" when riding. I think there's a message in this about the importance of motorcycle riding to one's mental health—being in the moment and focused on tasks enables your brain to stay engaged. I continue on my way. I've noticed the congestion increasing and I seem to be coming into more suburbia.

I take a quick left and look for my closest beach, I don't want to spend all day riding around towns and cities. My destination is Bulcock Beach, not the southernmost beach area, but it is an easy place to start and does look like the beginning of the exposed sandy beach fronts. Further south, I can see patches of sand interspersed with the green forests of mangrove trees.

Caloundra, sitting at the southern end of the Sunshine Coast, stretches from the northern tip of Bribie Island to Mooloolaba. Similar to the Gold Coast, I'm not particularly drawn to the segmented sandy beaches named after each suburb. Past Moffat Beach, it's straight to Mooloolaba.

The sand is spectacular, and the azure ocean inviting. All the beaches at this end of the coast are framed by small rocky headlands and golden, horseshoe-shaped sandy beaches. These aren't long, straight stretches of sand but smaller, secluded inlets—some developed with cafes and resorts, others preserved as parklands for picnics. It's the kind of scenery that graces the pages of international travel magazines.

As I ride through the beach suburbs, I see more and more bikes parked outside trendy cafes or car parks overlooking the beach. On the Sunshine Coast, custom cafe racers and modern classics are everywhere. I guess it's the modern form of cafe racing.

While cafe racing of old focused on speed records, today's cafe culture could herald a new style of motorcycle and a gentler type of rider. Now, cafes dot every street corner, and coffee vans are parked in every car park. Today's cafe racing culture is more akin to taking the kids to school than competing in the TT Isle of Man. Soon, I find myself riding back through the resort town of Mooloolaba.

The road that runs along the beachfront takes an upward direction as it goes over Alexandra Headland and down into Maroochydore. On the left of the road are high-rise accommodation buildings, cars are jam-packed all along the road, and on the right a beachfront walking track with stairs leading down to the beach. Maroochydore Beach continues after this rocky headland with a significant amount of parkland just behind the beach. This is a popular walking track and has great vantage points to look out over both Mooloolaba and Maroochydore to find the best waves for surfing. The water is a deep green, the waves curling offshore and barrelling along, perfect for surfing. There are hundreds of little dots, each a surfer who for some reason isn't working mid-week.

I arrive back early to find my campsite trashed, there is rubbish from my rubbish bag strewn across the site, my table has been up turned, and my biscuits packets have been pecked open. It's like the police have been ransacking my gear looking for drugs. Out of the corner of my eye, I see a small black and red figure, watching me from the bushes. It's one of those terrorist bush turkeys. Don't be fooled; bush turkeys are not your friends. They have been my nemesis throughout my travels, and this one has just declared war.

I clean up my campsite. Finding little bits of driftwood, I return fire on the turkeys, but they're too quick and we form an uneasy truce. I take the time during the cease-fire to relax on the beach before I get dinner from the local takeaway.

The next morning, I wake early to the sound of crashing waves. Lying on my stretcher, I savour the ambiance, in no rush to hit the road. Today's journey is short, and for the first time in a while, I'll be back on dirt tracks. I enjoy a coffee before the "parking lot" residents wake and the onshore breeze picks up.

I'm eager to escape the congested traffic of the Gold Coast, Brisbane, and Sunshine Coast regions. Packing up is swift, and soon Emu is ready to go. Exiting the Sunshine Coast is challenging; regardless of the road I choose, I invariably find myself heading towards the Sunshine Plaza shopping centre. At one point, I mistakenly ride into the parking area. It seems all roads lead to shopping centres. Fortunately, on my fifth attempt to leave, I stumble upon a Kawasaki dealer and buy a Garmin Bike GPS. When I eventually manage to fit this new device to Emu, I should no longer have navigation issues.

I'm riding to the Cooloola Recreation Reserve and Harry's Hut on the upper Noosa River. After a couple of exhausting days on the Sunshine Coast, I have just one more tourist area to visit. Of all the places, this is my favourite. It's considered one of Australia's premier seaside playgrounds, featuring the Noosa River and Noosa Beach. Although the Noosa River isn't particularly long, it boasts some intriguing features.

Rivers hold a majesty with a special place in the hearts of many of us. They can grow from a peaceful stream that slowly and steadily meanders along, to the raging and turbulent monsters that consume all in their path.

There are two parts to Noosa: the town of Noosa and Hastings Street. If you successfully manage to stay on the beach road, you will ride directly through the town of Noosa. Like all towns, it has essential shopping, like hair and beauty salons, fast food joints, convenience stores, and a selection of bottle shops and cafes. Continuing on, you'll ride over a hill and descend into one of the most congested streets on the Sunshine Coast—Hastings Street, a bustling hub of shopping and cafes. Here, amidst fast food outlets, are upmarket cafes, clothing stores, real estate offices, beauty therapies, and home decor shops, with surf and surfboard shops more prevalent than anywhere else. Accommodation options line either side of the street, from apartments to hotels. A continuous stream of traffic snakes through this small tourist strip, funnelled into a bottleneck by a car park and roundabout at the entrance.

I decided to navigate through the strip and look for a coffee spot. I found a small space to park Emu next to an appealing cafe. Small Vespa-motor scooters, equipped with surf racks and boards, were ubiquitous, a necessity in this chaotic setting where panel vans would be impractical. Piloted mostly by young, fit, tanned men and bikini-clad surf girls, these scooters weaved through the tourist traffic with ease. In this town, minimal attire was the norm, and both men and women seemed to compete over who could wear less.

I settled into a rustic chair, removed my touring jacket with its built-in body armour, feeling somewhat overdressed, and observed the unique local bike culture. After enjoying my coffee, as I was securing some gear, a young English backpacker parked his old Suzuki GT200 next to Emu. We chatted about travel, bikes, and work for a while. He was working at resorts during his travels around Australia and planned to ride down the East Coast on his modest bike. I wished him luck as he merged back into the traffic and disappeared. His little naked bike seemed out of place among the surfboard-carrying Vespas and insignificant next to Emu. It reminded me of my youth when I arrived in Melbourne from New Zealand with just 800 dollars and a bag of tools.

Does the despair and dissatisfaction that many people face in later life stem from not getting out and living our dreams as young people? When I was growing up and stepping out to explore the world, there was always a nagging thought I should be working or at least moving forward in my career. So even though I spent some time on the Gold Coast in my twenties, I didn't take the time to just be me. Both my parents were hard-working and encouraged my brothers and I to have a strong work ethic rather than drop out for a while and explore the world. This translated to a life of work and no play, which I guess got me to where I was when I started this journey.

After cooling down and recaffeinating, I crossed the road and found my way onto a wooden boardwalk along the beach. Looking north, the walkway is lined with resorts, coffee shops, cafes (if only Emu were a cafe racer), and the occasional massage tent. Beyond these, from where I had come, lies the internationally renowned Hastings Street. From this vantage point, you can see the long sandy stretch of beach extending from Noosa North Beach to the Cooloola Recreational Reserve and Rainbow Beach.

To the south stands Noosa National Park and Noosa Heads. You can drive to several famous beaches within the park, including the Fairy Pools, Hell's Gates, and Alexandria Bay, the latter being an unofficial nudist beach. Given that most young people wear very little anyway, the purpose of a nudist beach seems somewhat moot.

Like all point breaks, the surf rolls in around the headland and creates the perfect tubes. This is a great family beach and one for all the shoppers as well. It is very reminiscent of Coolangatta. It was getting hot and while I would love to have stayed here for a couple of days and just relax on the beach I wanted to get to Harry's Hut.

By the time I got back to Emu, I was sweating so much that I looked like I had been for a surf with all my gear on. I had one more stop in Noosa, a small reserve tucked into the end of Hastings Street. The reserve was once a popular caravan park but had been turned into a nature park to preserve its uniqueness. Ample car parks in the reserve provide access to both the Noosa Beach and the Noosa River. The Noosa River inlet is a tight squeeze for boats coming in or going out to sea and there's a very popular beach right at that point.

It would be easy to sit here for hours, letting the day unwind under the shade of a tree, watching small boats navigate the narrow channel entry. But I had a destination in mind and it was already early afternoon. I needed to get moving; there was still a dirt track to ride.

Chapter 21
Who Was Harry and Why Did He Build This Hut?

"No man ever steps in the same river twice, for it's not the same river and he's not the same man."

— Heraclitus

Noosa's a great place and I have really enjoyed my short time here, but it's time to continue my journey and get to my camp for the night. I go through the usual routine: keys, helmet, glasses and gloves, then fire up the engine. Emu is sounding good so we ride back down Hastings Street, through the annoying traffic jam and north. I'm heading inland following the river, first through Noosaville, then Tewantin, and eventually into the bushland areas just south of Gympie. Riding now seems much easier. I feel a weight has been lifted from my shoulders, the first time since Canungra. I was at last out of the hustle and bustle of the tourist strip. For the first time in five days, I relaxed and truly enjoyed the ride. The road twisted and turned, and for the most part, I rode under the shade of giant eucalypts and beach scrub.

The road started to climb, and I came across a sign saying, "This is not the road to Harry's Hut," which seemed like a strange road sign. I ignored it and carried on my way. No sooner had I climbed up the escarpment when I came across a road with a sign pointing down and to the right. This was the real Harry's Hut track.

My destination for the night is at the end of this track at a small national park camp ground on the magnificent Noosa Everglades. I had booked a site the previous day on the Queensland National Parks web site, for only six dollars fifty per night. The Noosa Everglades is one of two everglades in the world. The most well known is the Florida Everglades in the United States. An everglade is a body of water and flooded grassland with intersecting rivers or creeks.

They're both havens for all sorts of wildlife and are considered hotspots for ecological diversity. I had been to Harry's Hut once before on a kayaking adventure, my brother and I kayaked to the top camping sites, and then down to Lake Cootharaba. The lake is freshwater feeding from the Everglades, it opens up to several kilometres wide and is said to be shallow (about a metre in some places). This causes an interesting kayaking experience if the wind is up and it becomes choppy. The lake channels from Boreen Point into the Noosa River and flows to the sea.

The Everglades are known as the "River of Mirrors" when the river is glassed-out—meaning not a ripple on the water, usually in the early morning or late afternoon. The tannin-coloured water reflects light and everything, including your kayak, appears as if you are floating on a mirror. Having experienced this phenomenon personally, I can attest to how surreal it feels.

It's like sitting on a mirror; there's no sense of up or down, and it can become quite disorienting.

The track to Harry's Hut is pot-holed and muddy in sections, making it a challenge even for a good four-wheel drive, but on an adventure motorcycle, it's truly exhilarating. I bounced over potholes and allowed the back wheel to spin and drift around in controlled power slides, enjoying the thrill of being back on the dirt and acting like a kid again. That was, until I hit some small patches of sand and became acutely aware of the excessive weight from my touring setup.

I had just pulled into my camping spot and turned off the engine when I thought I heard another adventure bike, specifically another 650 single. They have a distinctive thumping noise, unlike the more technically focused twins. Just as I convinced myself it was my imagination, I heard it again, and rounding the corner came a fully outfitted DR650. At the controls was a bearded biker named Mike, greeting me with a broad New Zealand accent, "G'day Mate," he said. "Thought I heard another bike." If there was ever a quintessential adventure bike, it had to be Mike's DR650, equipped with a long-range tank, spare fuel, water canisters, and various pieces of equipment.

We talked for a bit then Mike said he had to go and find a site to dry his tent ("Stealth Camp") and off he went. Sometime later after putting my tent up and sorting my sleeping gear for the night, I was just sitting down to brew a coffee when Mike turned up again. We sat at the nearby table and he regaled me with his travel stories of riding around Queensland.

He's a granddad who came to Australia to meet his newest family member when COVID-19 hit and border restrictions were implemented. Stranded in Queensland, he embraced the true adventurer spirit, bought a bike, and hit the road. His travels took him to the Cape and then out to Cameron's Corner at the boundary of Queensland, New South Wales, and the Northern Territory. On his return, he unintentionally took a closed road from Cameron's Corner. The road was covered in sand and bulldust, and Mike had an accident and lay on the road for some time assessing his injuries, but apart from a few bruises he and the bike were unharmed. It was then he realised he hadn't seen another vehicle all day. After picking himself up and dusting off, he reached the end of the road where a sign announced it was closed.

This highlights the dangers in solo travel in some parts of Queensland. Help can be a long way away and many of the roads out west see very little if any traffic for days. Most solo adventure riders are aware of this and carry a Personal Locator Beacon (PLB) with them. I have one attached to the strap on my backpack. In the case of a life-threatening emergency and provided I'm conscious, I will extend the aerial and push the big red button. This sends a signal to "International Rescue" and, hopefully, they send a helicopter, although in the outback this might take some time.

As we talked, I learnt more about his adventures, not just in Australia but all over the world. Once an adventurer, always an adventurer. I've often said it's the interesting people you meet that make travelling an amazing experience. Meeting Mike was one of the highlights of this trip.

Later that evening, I wandered over to Mikes's tent drying spot and offered him a glass (plastic cup) of red. However, he's a bourbon man, so I sipped on a red, he on his bourbon. His next stop was Brisbane, while I was headed in the opposite direction to Rainbow Beach. We exchanged tips on navigation routes and road conditions. Mike had just come from Rainbow Beach and shared his experiences and what to watch out for on the track. During our conversation, he asked how long it took me to pack up my gear. I hadn't thought about it before, but I guessed it's close to two hours. He laughed and said, "I'm closer to three, but I'm not in a hurry. Besides, there's a few cups of coffee to consider during packing." It's an adventure rider thing—the day doesn't start until the first cup of coffee.

I laughed, this was the same routine I had settled into: start packing, have a coffee, and repeat until you've had too much coffee or your gear is finally packed. The next morning, after packing my gear, I wandered back to his tent drying site, and he shared with me one of his percolated coffee creations. The percolator was one of those essential items that Mike carried, just like my BioLite stove.

We spent some time looking around Harry's Hut. This old wooden fishing hut sits at the entrance to the camping ground on the banks of the river. It is in a secluded area, just off the road. Sub-tropical trees hug the ancient wooden panels and large clumps of bamboo act like matinee curtains to the river just beyond the old veranda. It was built here as a fishing hut before the national park was declared. The original builder was a dentist in Gympie, who put the track through to it, upon his death he willed it to the state. What a beautiful spot to have your own private fishing shack.

If you're interested in kayaking, then paddling up the Noosa River is a must. The Upper Noosa River and the Noosa Everglades are hidden secrets of the Sunshine Coast. You can launch your kayak or paddle board of choice from Harry's Hut and paddle up to 10 designated camping sites. You can also get a motorboat up as far as Camp Three, but kayaking is king on this river.

If you're a dedicated kayaker, a Noosa River trip should definitely be on your list. You can start from either Harry's Hut or Boreen Point. There's a small campground at Boreen Point, but be warned: if you're crossing Lake Cootharaba, it's best to start early before the wind picks up. The lake is quite shallow and can become choppy in windy conditions. Once you find the entry to the Everglades, you'll come across an unmanned information kiosk. Just a few paddle strokes further and you'll reach Camp One, a well-maintained campground. Like all campgrounds in this area, you must book and pay the fee in advance. They offer toilets but no showers; if you need to clean up, you'll have to take a dip in the river.

Chapter 22
Chasing the Rainbow Serpent

In the quiet of the early morning, rustling in the leaf litter outside my tent wakes me. The sun is beginning to turn night into day, and it feels cold. Hearing more rustling from the other side of the tent, I pull on my jeans and slowly roll down the zipper of the tent, trying to be quiet and avoid provoking whatever is out there. Peering out through the slit I've created in the inner tent, I shine my head torch in the direction of the noise and spot the sleek lines of a massive lizard. Standing just metres from Emu, it's about two metres in length from tail to snout. This Lace Monitor, or Tree Goanna, is one of Australia's largest predatory lizards, only slightly smaller than the Perenti, the Asian water monitor, and the Komodo dragon of Indonesia.

Harry's Hut is known for these giant cold-blooded creatures. I was last here during the summer a few years ago, they were everywhere, sauntering through the campground, indifferent to human presence. They can be dangerous; without fear of humans, they will attack if provoked. I've seen two giant goannas fighting—it's a fierce sight.

It sees me and decides to slowly move away. Once it gets across the track, I feel brave enough to get out of my tent. The second lizard, smaller than the first, doesn't linger and quickly scurries off into the bush.

They hold a special place in the hearts of Aboriginal Australians. Ancient stories tell of heroic battles between Dirawong and the Rainbow Serpent. Dirawong is the teacher and protector of humans. It is often said that where there is a goanna, you will not find a snake, as the two are mortal enemies.

Snakes and goannas play a huge role in Aboriginal mythology. The Rainbow Serpent is an important part of the Aboriginal creation myth. I understand Aboriginal people would follow the rainbow to find waterholes.

The rainbow is seen as both a bringer and destroyer of life. As I look out over the Noosa Everglades and just above the horizon, I see a rainbow and wonder to myself if the serpent is looking after me today.

My destination today is Inskip Point, north of Rainbow Beach and opposite the famous Fraser Island. But before I can get there, I will ride over several sandy logging tracks to Rainbow Beach. The very name Rainbow Beach is synonymous with the creation myth.

Originally named Black Rock, it was renamed Rainbow Beach after Europeans discovered the coloured mineral sands. However, local Aboriginals have long known this area as the home of the Rainbow Serpent.

The beach is a favourite destination for sand-driving four-wheel-drive enthusiasts. There are access tracks from north of the Noosa River through to Rainbow Beach.

After dropping by at Mike's drying spot and wishing him safe riding, I rode out of the park heading for Rainbow Beach. A few days later, I received a message from Mike. He had successfully found a place to dry his tent near Brisbane and was about to visit his grandson. Later, I saw on his Facebook page that he had found work driving trucks in Central Queensland and was planning to return to New Zealand after his contract ended. Mike is one of those inspirational people you meet on the road. Not necessarily because they are doing extraordinary things, but because they approach life with a positive, can-do attitude. The last I heard, he was back in New Zealand.

The ride from Harry's Hut is not difficult. There are sandy patches and big potholes. Some sections are low-lying and hold onto water, making a series of slippery muddy patches, but nothing of too much concern.

Before long, I'm climbing up a steep dirt hill that marks the start of the Harry's Hut track, leading to the top of a pine logging plantation. I turn right and am immediately greeted by a large sign warning that the track is dangerous and only suitable for four-wheel drives. It would have been reassuring if it had included "and motorbikes." Navigating these tracks is challenging, and at least once I had to backtrack for 10 minutes after taking a wrong turn.

Mike had warned me about a small section of deep sand. I would like to say I twisted the throttle, pulled back on the handlebars, accelerated to cruising speed, and channelled my inner Toby Price, but the reality is quite the opposite, despite my previous exploits on the Dawson Development Road.

I took a more cautious approach, putting Emu into first gear, put both my feet out, shifted my weight back as far as I could and jumped Emu headlong into the fray. Keeping my revs up, pushing along when it got bogged down with my feet and generally manhandling the bike through. A couple of smaller sections like this and some sand towards the end and before I knew it, I was coming out of the beachside undergrowth onto the Rainbow Beach access road.

There are two towns or suburbs that make up this section of the Queensland coastal landscape, Rainbow Beach, and Tin Can Bay. I had heard a lot about Rainbow Beach over the years and was always interested in coming here to see the coloured sands.

To get to Rainbow Beach, you can come in via the road network from Gympie, over the logging track like I did, or up the beach from Noosa Northern Beaches. To come up via the beach, you have to judge the tides and be good at beach and sand riding. However, as I was riding a fully loaded adventure bike and very inexperienced with beach riding, this wasn't an option for me.

It is possible to ride these beaches on dirt bikes, and many people do. The tides on either side of Double Island Point can be unforgiving if caught at the wrong time, potentially leading to trouble. There's also a track crossing from Double Island Point to Rainbow Beach known as the Leisha Track, famed for its deep, unforgiving sand.

As I stood looking back towards Double Island Point, an old KTM600 raced along the beach and up the well-worn sand ramp—clearly a very good rider, and riding a bike perfectly suited to the conditions.

Unfortunately, Emu, fully loaded, weighs approximately 250 kilograms, and I weigh 120, bringing our combined weight to 370 kilograms. We were acutely aware that riding down the beach was not going to happen for us on this trip.

The area has an infamous history. On July 7, 1973, the 1,600-ton coastal freighter *Cherry Venture* was navigating north when it encountered winds of 125 kilometres per hour and waves over 12 metres high. The ship's lack of cargo, compounded by these harsh weather conditions, is said to have led to its beaching. The wreck, located about three kilometres south of Double Island Point on Teewah Beach, became a popular tourist site for many years. Salvage attempts failed, and it wasn't until 1985 that the ship was dismantled and its propeller relocated to a park overlooking Rainbow Beach. Today, it stands as a monument and a significant reminder of the maritime history of the region.

I was eager to reach my camping destination for the night but I wanted to take a look at the neighbouring town of Tin Can Bay. After exploring the Rainbow beach, which consist of a pub, surf life-saving club, caravan park, and a few shops, I headed down the undulating tar-sealed track, turning right at the intersection leading to Tin Can Bay. Tin Can Bay has a different feel to it. While Rainbow Beach is the hip, young, family-friendly town, and 4x4 destination. Tin Can Bay is a more sedate fishing village with a boating and retirement culture, it is nestled in a protected anchorage at the beginning of the Great Sandy Strait.

The bay itself is inland and provides a safe harbour for boats entering the strait. The strait is between Fraser Island and the mainland at the end of the Cape, which is Inskip Point. It is one of the most tranquil places I have been so far on the east coast of Queensland. The ride from Rainbow Beach was also great for a motorcycle with its sealed roads and sweeping corners. On each side are sand dunes and low salt bush shrubbery. It took about 45 minutes, but compared to my ride through Brisbane, it was relaxing and lots of fun.

By the time I got to Tin Can Bay, I needed a break, so I stopped for coffee at the local park on the point near the northeast passage and opposite the wetlands. I enjoyed watching the birdlife, so I pulled out my cooking gear and made my coffee. From the park's picnic tables, I could see over the tranquil inlet to the Ramsar Convention Wetland, an internationally important area for birds. Pelicans were floating by and all sorts of other birds diving and twisting in the sea breeze.

My intention today was to get to back to Inskip Point, set up camp, and then take some photos of the beaches on the point. This would be the last beach in this area before continuing my journey north towards Harvey Bay in the morning. I filled Emu up at the petrol station and continued to Inskip Point.

Inskip Point is at the southern end of the Great Sandy Strait, where the mainland curves around into the strait. It is the southern access point for the Fraser Island barge. I've been here once before. At the time, I was intrigued by the camping sites just back from the beach, behind the dunes. So on this trip, I decided to camp there. Being a national park, you should book a camping spot using the National Parks website. I booked my site at the same time as I booked the camping ground at Harry's Hut, probably the cheapest camping you will get anywhere at $6.50 per night.

The trip out from Rainbow Beach was a pleasant tar-sealed road. There are campsites all up the peninsular, each marked with different names. It pays to try and remember the name allocated to you. I'm still not sure I camped where I said I would, but it didn't seem to matter in the end.

When I rode into one of the far sites, I instantly felt comfortable. The sand was rather deep and there were many grey nomad vans scattered among the small beach trees and scrub. People were sitting together enjoying a beer or wine and interacting. I managed to find a small area between a couple of trees that provided shelter from vehicles coming in at night.

After setting up my tent, some friendly neighbours came over and we talked about camping and travelling. There is a camaraderie between travellers that gives you a chance to meet interesting and memorable people. My neighbours were the most interesting people that I had met since leaving the outback.

They invited me for dinner and a couple of glasses of wine. We spend the night talking about grave digging and ghosts. My host, Damien, was a grave digger who had some interesting stories about digging up graves in the middle of the night during a thunderstorm, only to accidentally break through one coffin to find it lead-lined with a perfectly preserved body inside. According to Damien, lead is used if the person died of a influenza or an incurable virus. They quickly covered up the grave and reported it to the council; however, the council had no record of the body and of course, no idea why it was lead-lined.

I could have stayed here for several days; it was such a peaceful and comfortable campsite. As the afternoon wore on, clouds started to roll in, and it looked like it might rain. The campground was well set up, with patches of soft flat sand between small beach scrubs where you could park your van or set up your tent, surrounded by deep sand gullies with giant wheel tracks. It's protected from sea squalls and blowing sand by the sand dunes near the water.

I went onto the beach to take some photos of Fraser Island. The sea was turbulent, with white caps right across the passage as the wind fought back against the outgoing tide. I felt cold, so I zipped up my jacket and shivered slightly against the sudden chill. The conditions weren't ideal for photography, and I struggled to capture the aggressive nature of the landscape. As a storm seemed to roll in, I headed back to my tent to make sure it was securely tied down with enough guy ropes. Just as I was leaving, I saw the faint formation of a rainbow—it seemed the serpent was on the move again.

This was one absolute adventure-filled day. It started with my meeting with the rainbow serpent and ended up talking about grave digging. I am looking forward to a good night's sleep.

Chapter 23
Riding the Great Sandy Strait

> "My dream is to have a house on the beach, even just a little shack somewhere so I can wake up, have coffee, look at dolphins, be quiet and breathe the air."
>
> — Christina Applegate

The Great Sandy Strait is a navigable channel that stretches from Inskip Point to Sandy Cape on the northeastern tip of Fraser Island near Hervey Bay. It's the channel between the mainland and Fraser Island now renamed K'Gari. The combination of the Great Sandy Straits and azure seas provides a pristine environment for fishing.

I awoke this morning to the usual sounds of a campground: early rising anglers (apparently the early bird does catch the worm), the aromatic smell of bacon and eggs cooking on a barbecue somewhere upwind, children talking, and the faint sound of a small dog barking. Lying in my cot, I took in the sounds and smells, watching the shadows of tree branches dance across my tent fly. It was a peaceful, tranquil moment, but I needed to capture a sunrise photo of the beach. Rolling off my stretcher, I banged my knee on the floor.

With my jeans half-zipped, I managed to open the tent flap while cursing about my knee, and flopped out unceremoniously, clipping the tent doors as I went. After standing up and dusting myself off, I took one step and tripped over my camping chair, swearing and hobbling, I looked around to see if anyone had noticed. Situation-normal. I found myself standing up again, taking a deep breath I thought to myself, another graceful exit from my tent. I'm starting to get good at this camping stuff.

The main attraction here is Fraser Island, but for anglers, it's the nutrient-rich, mangrove-lined shores that serve as breeding grounds for an assortment of fish and crustaceans. Most people catch the barge here to get to the southern point of the island, drive up the beach, and catch the ferry to Hervey Bay. It would be an amazing adventure to take the barge across and ride up the golden sands. However, I was on a heavy touring bike, and riding along the Fraser Island beach was not feasible—I could see myself riding off the barge and immediately sinking up to my bash plate. The newspaper headlines would read "Intrepid Adventurer Bogged on Launch Ramp." To avoid embarrassment and not provide ammunition for my esteemed colleagues, I chose the path less travelled and decided to ride parallel to the Great Sandy Strait, checking out some of the beach communities along the way.

The first part of my ride is back to Rainbow Beach. It's time to fuel up at the Tin Can Bay petrol station. As I'm filling the tank, an older guy walks past wearing a leather racing jacket, denim jeans, and motorcycle riding boots. With his gray hair and long beard, he introduces himself as Peter. I ask him what he's riding and he points to a pristine Aprilia RS 1000 V4 parked at the front pump, adorned in Aprilia Racing's white, green, and red. His helmet matches the bike, but Peter, is the odd one out, he's thin and elderly, and seems a contrast to his sporty ensemble.

We stand and talk for a while. He lives at Tin Can Bay but is just racing down to Brisbane to spend some time with his grandson. He's been riding all his life and loves the feeling of getting out on the highway. At 78, he's not thinking of slowing down just yet. It's time to continue and I wish him safe riding. He tips his helmet and then races up the hill, lifting the front wheel as he goes.

It occurs to me that Peter obviously understands the importance of staying active and doing what you love, rather than conforming to social norms, like working until you drop dead. Most older people I have talked to in their late seventies are starting to slow down, driving becomes more difficult and the things they could once do easily, seem so much harder. They decide that they should wind back their activities, and then they age.

My father rode an R1150 RS BMW until he was 74. After a friend got injured in a freak accident, he stopped riding out of fear he might sustain an injury. At the time, I said to him instead of stopping, why not consider getting a lighter bike or as a toolmaking engineer and ex-cafe racer, perhaps take up restoring old bikes? For the rest of his life, he lamented his riding career and motorbikes in general but never got back on one. He retired from engineering at 84 years of age and passed away eight years later.

I seem to have discovered another of those life lessons and my encounter with Peter reinforces it, that age shouldn't be a barrier to enjoying life—it's all about mindset, as the saying goes, "Whether we believe we can or can't, we're right."

As I continue riding, a cold, moist wind seeps through my jacket, chilling me. I pass through pine plantations, feeling like an intruder in the sombre landscape. The overcast sky and mundane traffic transform today's ride, making it feel more like a commute to work than an adventure—it's the first time in 18 days I've felt this way.

The beach communities from Tin Can Bay to Hervey Bay seem to follow a consistent template: they are primarily fishing communities. Each one features similar waterfront styles and leads onto the Great Sandy Straits. They boast an assortment of shops, caravan parks, and small but functional community centres. There appears to be a proliferation of retirees, as modern houses emerge among the old fibro fishing shacks. I don't linger long in these areas; it's cold and windy, and without a bakery or coffee shop to retreat into and enjoy the ocean views, they feel bleak and uninviting. They might be lovely on a sunny, calm day, but today they are just grey and unwelcoming.

Before long, I'm back on the road looking for the turn-off to my next destination. I imagine in the summer it would be great to camp here, throw up a hammock, and throw out a fishing line for a few days. A bit like Huckleberry Finn with this bamboo fishing pole, looking out at a beautiful subtropical landscape.

My next destination is the timber town of Maryborough. It's often overlooked in the annals of Queensland's history tellers, but it had a significant impact on the development of Queensland. It's one of Queensland's oldest cities and was once home to a Queensland immigration centre. By 1860, it welcomed more than 23,000 immigrants from Europe (mainly England).

Established in 1847, it quickly grew to be a main centre for immigration and was declared a port in 1859. It was a major trading port for wool, timber, sugar cane, and gold. In 1925, a sawmill was established and many high-quality wood products were exported. Much has been said about the use of kanakas or indentured labour from the Pacific islands in Townsville and North Queensland generally, but this is where much of that trade started. There were over 12,000 kanakas brought into Maryborough to provide cheap (almost free) labour to the region. The practice was short-lived and was halted by 1903, due to it being considered a form of slavery.

Architecturally, the city showcases a mix of late classical and early Art Deco designs. Riding through Maryborough feels like moving through a living museum, reminiscent of the Art Deco architecture in Napier, New Zealand.

Every strategic port needs defences, and Maryborough Port is fortified with several cannons, more characteristic of World War One than 17th-century armaments, perched high on the riverbanks, though they likely haven't seen much action.

It was lunchtime when I arrived, and though I looked for a bakery, I settled for a fish and chip shop. I tucked the hot chips inside my jacket for warmth and found a nearby park to enjoy them. By the time I finished, it had started to rain, and the persistent cold wind made me even colder. Eager to continue, I revved up Emu and we headed towards Hervey Bay.

Back on the road, I zipped my jacket tight and pulled my scarf over my nose to protect my lips from chapping. The industrial buildings lining the road were dark and foreboding, reminiscent of my early days working in a factory in Dandenong, Victoria.

Hervey Bay had such an auspicious start to European history, so much so that Captain James Cook sailed around what was to become Fraser Island without realising it was an island. But to be fair, the waters of the Great Sandy Strait were not deep enough for the *Endeavour* to navigate, anyway. Therefore, Cook made a wise decision not to explore further. However, he did name the bay that stretched around to the south. It was called Hervey Bay on behalf of Britain's First Lord of the Admiralty at the time, Augustus Hervey.

It wasn't until 1802, when the great Matthew Flinders landed at Sandy Cape and mapped the area, that he realised there was an island in the middle of the bay. Surprisingly, Flinders did not name the island. It was not named until 1836, when Captain Fraser and his wife, survivors of a shipwreck, managed to land on it.

The more I read about Australia's early European history, the more I am saddened. What we see is often not what the first explorers saw. Neither did they walk the beautiful soft golden sand and sit to watch the sunset. They sailed past, but to be fair there were hostile conflicts between Europeans and Aboriginals, and while the Aboriginal peoples in this area were friendly, not all groups were.

Without a doubt, Harvey Bay is one of the jewels of the Fraser Coast. It boasts a thriving tourist community with exceptional beach frontage, interspersed with caravan parks, resorts, restaurants, and coffee shops almost every 10 metres.

Rather than take hundreds of photos of golden sand and azure waters, I rode from Urangan Pier at the southern point to Brennan Park at the northern end. There are golden beaches with tranquil waters all along this route.

As the afternoon progressed, I still had about an hour of riding left before I could stop for the night. I had arranged to meet up with some old friends for a couple of nights in Bundaberg.

Chapter 24
How Does a Polar Bear Promote Rum?

> "Thanks to the federal highway system, it's now possible to travel from coast to coast to coast without seeing anything."
> — Charles Kuralt

I've never really considered myself to be an adventurer, or that I would ever live the life of an adventurer. During parts of my life, I've met people who have travelled the world. Their stories seemed too exciting to be real, from one country to another with endless challenges faced and overcome. The amazing places they visited and the extraordinary people they met.

Each of these stories seemed like an extraordinary holiday, but when I reflect on those times, it occurred to me that the stories (or the holidays) were joined together by the journey narrative. It was this narrative that was exciting, what happened between the destinations. Like the time a friend of mine, "John the Ibis," was on a bus in Central America when a man pointed at his watch. John thought the man was asking for his watch and, feeling vulnerable in a strange land, started to remove it to avoid a potentially violent mugging. However, the man shook his head and said, "No, keep your watch hidden, man, and keep your arm inside the bus. The kids in the villages will jump up and rip it off and gouge your arm." It was a moment of compassion from one stranger to another, a rare kindness we don't often witness in our daily lives.

When I read *Jupiter's Travels* by Ted Simon, I got the feeling about halfway through Africa that something changed for Ted, he stopped being a tourist and became a traveller. He became more confident and he stopped giving a fuck about everything and just went with the flow.

I guess it takes time to fall into the life of an adventurer, a traveller's mentality that most of us only experience during an extended holiday. Now, 19 days into my journey on my trusty KLR650, this no longer feels like a holiday but rather an adventure. The initial 30 days planned don't seem long enough, and I'm already planning my next adventure and the modifications I'll need to make to Emu to prepare for it.

I arrived in Bundaberg mid-afternoon, luckily missing both school and peak traffic. Officially established in 1868, Bundaberg quickly became known for its sugar cane and timber industries. Situated on the Burnett River, the town developed into a bustling port and distribution centre, its architecture—late classical and early Art Deco from the late 1800s and early 1900s—reflecting its prosperous past.

When I think of Bundaberg, I think of two iconic things: Bundy Rum and turtles. A strange combination I hear you say, especially as my drink of choice is red wine. But I have always attributed Bundaberg with the flashy golden bottles, and for some reason, polar bears. Where the fuck did that come from, polar bears?

We're hardly in the Arctic Circle and it would be the last thing you think of in Central Queensland. I think the marketing genius who thought that up must have been dropped into a pit of fermenting sugar. While the rum is well known, at least in Australia, there is a little less known secret to the Bundaberg region in the way of sea turtles.

My first impression of Bundaberg is it's an industrial town. I was flanked by sugar cane fields and the smoking chimneys of the cane-crushing plants billowing out their superheated steam into a grey moist day. Eventually, I made my way to my friend's place, whom I hadn't seen in almost six years.

Sharing stories of my adventures, they seemed almost too unbelievable to be true, yet they were. My entire demeanour has shifted; I'm no longer just on holiday but traveling for the thrill of the journey itself, which has become as significant in my storytelling as the destinations I've visited.

Robin and Maranda are travellers too and spend as much time as they can visiting new places, some of which I had just visited. I was able to share my experiences and learn more about those places from them. Our storytelling went on into the night, and eventually, we became too tired to continue.

Waking this morning was a complete contrast to camping at Inskip Point. The usual morning light across the tent had changed to small gaps in the curtains. It was early and the house was quiet. I got up and made a coffee before moving to the veranda.

There is a paradox I've discovered in the life of an adventurer: you can go wherever you want with no set plan, which is a wonderfully unpredictable way to live. It allows the universe to make plans for you. The paradox is if you don't plan your journey, there's a good chance you will go around in circles and never really get anywhere. Yet, getting somewhere and enjoying the journey is the point of travelling. So, do you plan or not plan? It's still a mystery.

This brings me to today's activities: navigation. Navigation is crucial if you aim to reach a specific destination, unless you enjoy going around in circles. So far, my navigation had been less than stellar, but since I was mostly following one major road, it hadn't been a significant issue. Armed with a series of paper maps, I had navigated much of Queensland, though I admit to getting lost while trying to avoid toll roads in Brisbane.

To resolve this paradox, consider buying a GPS. Set your destination and let it guide you. Often, it will take you on the longest and most challenging route, providing all the adventurous detours you need. Thus, you enjoy both a unique and unpredictable journey and, eventually, reach your destination—just don't worry about arriving on time. Paradox solved.

On the Sunshine Coast, I found a motorcycle-specific GPS, the Garmin 396 LT, but lacked the tools to install it. When I mentioned this to Robin, he eagerly offered to help. He's the kind of person who enjoys helping and knows a lot about these things, so I happily accepted his assistance.

After stripping Emu down to the frame and installing a raft of new wires and fuses, we managed to get the engine running again with the GPS operational. Unfortunately, the bike battery was drained. Thinking it might have been something we did, we charged it overnight.

Remember I mentioned turtles earlier? Bundaberg is home to Mon Repos, one of the most famous sea turtle breeding beaches in Australia. Mon Repos, French for "My Rest," is the largest turtle rookery on Australia's east coast, located about nine kilometres north of Bundaberg. The beach and turtle centre are world-renowned for their success in breeding sea turtles. Most sea turtles in Australian waters are endangered, making Mon Repos's work extremely important. The beach is primarily visited by loggerhead and flatback turtles, who return annually to lay eggs. Occasionally, green and leatherback turtles have also nested here.

The name Mon Repos comes from a homestead established in 1884 by Angus Barton, a pioneer of the sugar industry in the region. Interestingly, the area was once owned by the French Government after a telephone cable being laid from New Caledonia came ashore here. Another notable fact is that one of the world's famous aviators and a favourite Bundaberg resident, Burt Hinkler, built and flew gliders from Mon Repos beach before becoming the first person to fly an airplane from England to Australia in 1928.

You could spend weeks in Bundaberg exploring its rich history, and if you visit the rum distillery, you might find yourself indulging in a few different vintages for a week. As comfortable as the queen-sized bed was, I was conscious not to overstay my welcome since I had many more beaches to photograph and places to visit. It was great catching up with Robin and Miranda. Fortunately, my bike started on the first try, which was a relief after the battery issues the previous afternoon.

The weather was overcast and threatening rain again, definitely not a fun day to be riding around town. It was time to leave, so after setting my course on my new GPS, I headed out of town. As I was heading north, the impressive engineering structure of the

Bundaberg Rail Bridge over the Burnett River came into view. I had to stop and take a picture of this engineering marvel.

It's day 20, and I'm on my way to Blue Water and then to the town of 1770. There's a direct road between the two areas, and I don't have to go back to the highway.

Chapter 24
Lieutenant James Cook RN was here 1770

"It's not so much for its beauty that the forest claims men's hearts, as for that subtle something, that quality of air that emanation from old trees, that so wonderfully changes and renews a weary spirit."
— **Robert Louis Stevenson**

I do risk management for a living, and I like to think I had identified the problems I would encounter on such a road trip, but I was not prepared for the unexpected drama that would befall me that day. This begs the question: How effective are our risk assessments if we can't predict all eventualities?

My journey yesterday was short, so I decided not to fill up in Bundaberg and continued the 168 kilometres to the town of 1770. I had about 200 kilometres worth of fuel in my tank, and as a result, I broke one of my golden rules: Never leave town without filling up.

I wanted to check out a free camping site at Rules Beach, but as I was now getting low on fuel, I thought the 40-kilometre round trip would be too much. By the time I reached the next petrol station, I decided to carry on and return to the free camping site later in the afternoon when I could pitch my tent.

I was keen to explore the beaches around 1770 and Agnes Waters, especially Chinaman's Beach. Many places in Australia are called "Chinaman's Beach," most attributed to anecdotal records of Chinese gold prospectors between 1870 and 1910. The Chinese mined sand from which they extracted gold, amounting to approximately 24 million dollars in today's currency from Chinaman's Beach in the region. However, the Immigration Restriction Act of 1901, known as the White Australia Policy, curtailed Chinese gold mining.

As you ride west from Agnes Waters to Chinaman's Beach, you will come across the sandy track entrance to Deep Water National Park. This track, usually firm but sandy, connects Rules Beach with Agnes Waters. Along the way, there are two main shaded camping areas, Middle Rock and Wreck Rock Camping.

These would have been great camping areas for the night, but the 17 kilometres of deep sand track was a little daunting on a fully loaded adventure bike. As a solo rider, the risk of getting stuck in the sand was too great. It might have been worth the risk if I were travelling with friends, but solo, getting bogged down was a risk I didn't want to take. The park is named after Deep Water Creek, which can be crossed at a causeway.

The mining and the Chinese have long vanished; the beach today is renowned as one of the few great surfing spots within the Great Barrier Reef Lagoon. Most beaches within the confines of the Great Barrier Reef lack any significant wind-blown swell and are too shallow for the development of a deep ocean surge.

On my last night in Bundaberg, I was telling Robin about snakes and how I hadn't seen many on this trip, partly due to it being the middle of winter and a little cold. Robin regaled me with a story of a massive king brown snake he saw on the road near Quilpie. He said it went from one side of the road to the other.

Interestingly, after talking about snakes, I encountered a king brown snake myself while riding back from Chinaman's Beach. I stopped a safe 200 metres away and took out my camera. This was the largest venomous snake I had ever seen, stretching across one lane of the road. Knowing that king browns are aggressive and highly venomous, I waited until it had completely crossed the road before continuing. Afterwards, I headed down to the beach at Agnes Waters and bought a coffee from the local cafe. The more I explored Agnes Waters, the more appealing it seemed as a great place for a family holiday.

After visiting the beaches and coffee shops of Agnes Waters, I rode to the township of 1770. From Agnes Waters, you turn left at the Caltex petrol station and follow the winding road until you reach the Round Hill Creek Estuary. You are now in 1770. Continue past a small pub, a coffee shop, and a bakery until you reach Round Hill Headland. Several modern houses on the hill overlook Bustard Bay. Halfway up, you'll find the monument to Captain James Cook's second landing in Australia.

The anniversary of Cook's historic landing is celebrated with a festival each year. The town's name, 1770, clearly capitalises on this historical event.

I refer to Captain James Cook RN because, although he served as a lieutenant in the Royal Navy during this expedition, it was customary to address the commander of the ship as Captain. In later years, he would be promoted to Captain of Captains, a particularly high command, especially for someone of common birth.

The 1770 Caravan Park, nestled just below the monument to Captain Cook, is likely very close to where the crew of the *Endeavour* landed in 1770. Surrounded by majestic palms, it's arguably one of the most picturesque caravan parks in the state, overlooking the famous inlet which offers sheltered swimming and access for small boats. I couldn't linger long, though, as it was nearing late afternoon.

I spent some time at the picnic grounds in front of the caravan park, intending later to camp at Rules Beach. With a full tank, I packed up and headed south. Unfortunately, the free camping ground at Rules Beach was 500 metres up the beach, and by the time I arrived, the tide was high, lapping at the soft dunes. With no other option, I rode back towards 1770, looking for a suitable site along the way.

About five kilometres before Agnes Waters, I rode past a small park with some camper vans in it. To my surprise, it was a well-set-up and maintained campground. The owners were ex-Northern Territory National Park rangers and were very friendly. The park is known as "Travellers Rest" and is a great place to stay the night. I had a peaceful sleep with very little traffic noise and no wild parties. The only exception to this was the noisy opossum in the tree next to my tent.

The next day, I had a leisurely breakfast of muesli, a couple of cups of coffee with two servings of cheese and biscuits and went for a hot shower to wash away yesterday's road grime.

Today is day 21 of my motorcycle adventure and everything seemed normal. I was going to ride along the highway today for a few hours, so I wasn't prepared mentally for the unexpected drama I was about to face. I planned to head up the coast to Rockhampton and then to the beaches of Yeppoon, dropping into Gladstone to photograph the beach suburb of Tannum Sands along the way. Gladstone always seems very industrial to me, with the aluminium smelter, coal terminals, and coal-fired power station making up most of the scenic backdrop to the town.

I was also looking forward to catching up with my niece and her husband in Yeppoon. Packing had become routine, and I was ready to ride in no time. I went through the usual routine, helmet, sunglasses, gloves on, glove off pull the key out of my jeans, glove back on and pressed the start button, nothing happened. The electrical system was dead, not even a click. Repeated attempts to start the bike failed. I checked the kickstand sensor; I was in neutral but still, nothing. It wasn't mechanical; it had been running fine the night before. Fuel flow was normal, so it wasn't fuel-related. There was simply no spark. I checked the spark plug, the lead, and even went through all the connections. Everything seemed fine, including the fuses under the seat.

I suspected what the problem was; this unexpected drama seemed to be a continuation of the issue Robin and I assumed was just a drained battery. Now, it appeared much worse. Rather than merely going flat in Bundaberg, the battery was on its way out and had chosen this moment to fail completely.

Thoughts of being stranded miles from anywhere with a potential replacement 12-volt motorcycle battery flooded my mind. How long would I have to wait for a delivery from the nearest dealer? And where was the nearest dealer?

One reason I opted for the 2018 model, despite a new model being imminent, was my comfort in handling such unexpected issues, like a fuel problem. Emu had a carburettor instead of a fuel injection system, and its electronics were relatively simple. As someone who spent 15 years as an engineering tradesperson and much of my youth working on cars and bikes, I understand mechanical systems. A carburettor performs a similar function to the modern bike's fuel injection and pump system, but it uses gravity to feed fuel into the carburettor, then, through a pressure diaphragm and a jet, the fuel is atomised and injected into the piston. As the piston compresses and is ignited by the spark plug, the resulting explosion forces the piston down, generating power to the wheels.

The advantage of having carburettors over a fuel pump and fuel injection system is that it doesn't require electricity to start a carburettor bike; I can push-start it. If I only could push the bike fast enough, the generator, which normally feeds power to the battery, would develop enough spark to start the bike and by pushing the bike in gear you would provide the compression of the fuel to ignite it.

Fortunately, I found a couple of fit-looking fishermen (another oxymoron) at the camping spot opposite me who were willing to help push me to ignition speed. After all, I'm one of the 90% of people who subsidise their fishing gear while managing not to catch a single fish. I put the bike in second gear and waited until we were going fast enough, then released the clutch lever and bingo, Emu kicked into life. Once the motor was running, it would produce enough charge to keep going for a while. I thanked my helpers and set off to find the nearest Kawasaki dealer for a new battery.

I had planned a detour to Gladstone, but with the battery issue, all I wanted was to reach the dealer and replace it. It's about 200 kilometres to Rockhampton, so I would need to stop for fuel at Miriam Vale and hope Emu had enough charge to restart.

Miriam Vale was bustling with activity on the Bruce Highway, filled with grey nomads and bikers of all types. Next to some tables on the grassy area, there was a group of around eight Harley touring bikes, most with a pillion passenger. I figured they would help if I needed a push. After all, it's the number one rule of the biker's code of conduct: Never leave a fellow biker stranded on the side of the road.

After paying for my fuel, I went through the ritual of donning my helmet, grabbing my keys, putting on my glasses, and slipping on my gloves. Turning the ignition, I pushed the starter, but all I got was a rhythmic clicking noise. Although the battery had held a small charge, it wasn't enough to start the bike. Fortunately, a fit-looking young Harley rider was passing by, so I called out for help. He glanced at his mates before agreeing to give me a push. I rolled off the forecourt, and after a couple of seconds, I let the clutch go. The bike rumbled a few times but didn't start. I just needed a little more speed. As I turned back to my assistant to say, "Just one more push should do it," I noticed he had left and was mounting his Harley. It seemed he might not fully understand the biker code of conduct.

Sure, helping out might slow you down, but isn't it better to have helped someone than to arrive precisely on time at your next destination? Seriously, the universe doesn't care if you're five minutes late.

As a kid, I remember my father would always stop if someone was broken down on the side of the road. He was an engineer and more often than not he could get their car going. For someone to walk off before the job was done, was a little rude. It says something about values. It's definitely not in the spirit of the "Biker Code of Conduct."

I was about to get off my bike to push when a middle-aged guy jumped out of his family four-wheel drive and asked if he could help. I gladly accepted, and within seconds, Emu was purring again. We talked for a couple of minutes about adventure travel. It turns out he was travelling with his family but had always wanted to tour on a motorbike. I wonder if our conversation led to him getting another bike, the universe is funny like that.

I wished him safe travels and hit the highway. It started to rain and I could feel the moisture seeping through the outer layer of my adventure jacket. The light grey clouds I had left in 1770 were now starting to thicken into a dark blurry mass that seemed to get heavier the further north I travelled. I zipped up my jacket and mentally prepared for the onslaught and a cold wet ride to Rockhampton.

At Calliope, the clouds burst and the rain pummelled me big time. I found a small rest area where I took refuge under a covered table and searched Emu for my rain jacket. I was conscious not to stop the engine as I fumbled through the panniers. No sooner had I got back on the road than the rain stopped. By the time I got to Rockhampton, it was sunny and hot again.

Emu was only six months old, a mere baby chick, so when I pulled into the Rockhampton Kawasaki dealer, I was hopeful for at least a new battery, or perhaps some assistance installing one. Luckily, they had a new glass plate battery in stock. It was also time to replace my tires, as I had covered over 7,000 kilometres on the original ones. I received a quote for a set of Mitas S70 tyres. The battery was priced at 120 dollars, and although initially informed there was no warranty, I later discovered otherwise.

However, the most disappointing aspect of this visit was the poor customer service; they were too busy to install the battery or tyres for another week.

I could use their workshop to change the battery myself, but they wouldn't allow me access to their tire-changing equipment. After purchasing the battery, I installed it myself in their workshop—a straightforward task that took about 15 minutes after removing all the necessary parts and the seat. Emu started immediately after installation, and I asked a mechanic to check the bike's charging system, which he confirmed was functioning well. Eager to leave, I soon departed the dealership.

Rockhampton is situated along the Fitzroy River, fed by several inland waterways, including the Dawson, Comet, and Mackenzie Rivers. I had ridden over the headwaters of this river system early in my outback adventure. The creek I crossed on my way to Black Alley Peak is one of the sources of the Comet River, which eventually flows into the Fitzroy River.

The Fitzroy River basin spans 142,665 square kilometres, making it the largest river system on the eastern coast of Australia. It empties into Keppel Bay, south of Emu Park, between Thompson Point and Port Alma. Now with a new battery, Emu seemed much happier, so instead of lingering in Rockhampton, we headed to his namesake town, Emu Park. On the way, I wanted to explore Keppel Sands, a small community located just south of Emu Park.

Keppel Sands is located just south of Emu Park. In front of the small community is a long park and an even longer sandy beach with its southern end at the mouth of the Fitzroy River. The beach connects to a shallow mud flat at low tide, with a long and wide ribbon of sandy mud.

I've been told that crocodiles can be spotted on the beach during the summer months when the air temperature is higher than the water temperature. There was a sense of calm as I rode out from Keppel Sands, it felt like I was flowing through a subtropical beachside forest with small lagoons and towering pandanus palms everywhere.

Riding into Emu Park I felt my stomach rumble. It was mid-afternoon and I hadn't eaten since about six o'clock this morning. With all the unexpected drama of the day, I had completely forgotten to eat. Luck would have it, I found a bakery and I was able to stock up on a steak pie and sausage roll before I headed to a small beachside park to make a coffee.

The first recorded European settlement in this area was when grazier John Jardine established a cattle property in 1860. However, Captain Cook sailed past in 1770, naming the bay, "Keppel Bay" after Admiral Augustus Keppel of the British Royal Navy. It must have been spectacular for him and his crew as he entered the tranquil azure waters of what was to be named The Great Barrier Reef.

Emu Park became a holiday place in the 1870s when the affluent residents of Rockhampton established holiday homes in the area overlooking Pine and Fisherman's beaches. Today, it continues as a holiday destination but is significantly less developed compared to Yeppoon. Overlooking Keppel Bay, perched on top of Constitution Hill, is Churchill Lookout. At the lookout is a monument called "Singing Ship Monument." It commemorates Captain Cooks's voyage through Keppel Bay in May 1770.

The ride from Emu Park to Yeppoon is spectacular as it swerves in and out from beach to beach. I had forgotten the unexpected drama of this morning, as I passed yet another golden ribbon of stunning beach. The golden sand that demarcated the bright blue ocean from the green shrubbery made for a spectacular vista as I rode along the beachside between villages and then up over headlands. I found myself drifting into a deep sense of awe as I leaned into the corners and accelerated up the hills, only to come over the top and see the beautiful seascape of the tropics in front of me again. This is yet another moment in my list of positive reels that lift my spirits.

I was looking for a place to camp for the night and while I passed several suitable camping sites. I wanted to look around before settling down for the night.

It was four o'clock when I arrived at Yeppoon. The light was fading, as it does at this time in winter. I rode over the small hill that opened up to a salty inlet, and as I looked back, I saw fishing boats moored at the small inlet next to the inlet walls sitting on the dry sand, waiting for the tide to turn and float them for another fishing expedition. I saw a sign for the Yeppoon Caravan Park. That will do, I said to myself.

After paying a thirty five-dollar camping fee, I found a comfortable, unpowered grass site. I was looking forward to washing clothes, drying them, and enjoying a hot shower. Despite the morning's unexpected events, the day ended peacefully. The clear sky turned to inky blue silk, silently enveloping the last golden rays of the sun, promising excellent conditions for photography in the morning.

Chapter 25
Back in the Tropics

Once you step over the Tropic of Capricorn, you are back in the tropics. Interestingly, I'm geographically on the same latitudinal plane as I was in Longreach. I think there's a subtle change in the way life moves in the tropics. It seems slower, less concerned with the frantic pace of man-made mechanisms and more in tune with the slow rhythmic sway of palm trees.

There's a warm saltiness in the air, a sensation you can taste and feel on your skin that seems to open your pores and draw in the moist air. The light also appears different, possibly due to the presence of more palm and coconut trees and plants with large, broad leaves.

I rose from my camp stretcher, trying to be as quiet as possible as the sun was still an hour away from rising and even the local birds were still asleep. I was conscious to be as quiet as possible, pulling on my jeans and searching around for my down jacket. It was colder than I thought it would be; after all, we're in the tropics for fuck's sake, it's not meant to be cold. I quietly pulled the zipper on the tent. Have you ever noticed how loud the opening of a zipper sounds when you're trying to be quiet in the early morning? Each little plastic zip echoes across the campground. Is it better to zip it one lug at a time or just rip the thing down and be done with it?

While exiting my tent, I accidentally knocked over my table, scattering my pot, stove, and spare water across the grass. As I stood up, my head hit the top of the tent, and I stumbled back, tripping over the now-upturned table and cursing my clumsiness. During this commotion, a small dog appeared, seemingly amused by my antics, before it began barking loudly, awakening several campers as lights flickered on in nearby caravans. In my rush to escape the scene, I grabbed my camera and quickly left. All this happened before I even had my first cup of coffee.

To set the scene a little better, I had a sore toe from tripping over the table, I had woken the whole campsite by scaring a small dog, and I was now wandering around the urban part of Yeppoon without direction or caffeine. As I was lamenting the evil nature of the universe, I saw a vision of Biblical proportions; it was like a gleaming star or oasis in the desert. The bright lights in an otherwise dull-lit suburbia beaconed me like a moth to the camp lights. Right in front of me was the "Two Sisters" coffee shop and it was open. If that's not evidence of a divine power in the universe, I don't know what is.

Talking with my fellow coffee addicts I learnt I was at Cooee Bay. If I had turned around, I would have seen the great big fish and chip shop with the "Cooee Bay Takeaway" sign. I was going in the right direction to find the actual beach.

Soon, I climbed a small escarpment flanked by upscale homes with views over Cooee Bay. It was an excellent spot for photography and to enjoy my coffee while reflecting on the universe's vastness, my earlier grievances fading with each sip. I continued onto the beach at Cooee Bay, heading north as the sun began to rise, marking the sand with the first footprints of the day. The sunrise painted the sky in hues of crimson. Reaching the far side, I passed boats I had seen earlier resting on the sand.

I discovered a quaint cafe next to an impressive public pool known as the Yeppoon Lagoon. Settling onto a plastic sun chair, I sipped my second coffee of the day while observing people swimming laps in the lagoon as the sun climbed higher. The chill of the morning had dissipated, and I soon found myself overheating in my down jacket—a typical morning in the tropics, even in mid-winter.

The pool was a hub of activity, where people gathered for morning exercise and to enjoy their favourite beverages. Just down the foreshore and on prime beach frontage, I came across the Keppel Bay Sailing Club.

The sun had well and truly up by the time I walked back to the caravan park. I needed to get back on the road. I was meeting my niece and her husband at the local "Coffee club." A fitting place considering my coffee addiction. The name "Coffee Club" always makes me think of Alcoholics Anonymous: "Hello, my name's Gary, I've been addicted to coffee since I was eight years old. It has been one hour, 23 minutes, and 32 seconds since my last cup," at which point everybody would applaud and we would go on to the next person.

After following the directions my niece provided, I found the local shopping centre and rode down into the underground car park. Finding the most conspicuous location, I parked Emu and locked the front wheel with my ear-piercing (125 db) brake alarm. My niece and her husband are Savannah Guides, who at the time were working at the Capricorn Caves.

They weren't starting work until later in the day; it was an opportunity to catch up on all the gossip. They mentioned a quick route north that involved a couple of dirt roads that would bring me out to the Capricorn Caves and bypass the early weekday traffic around Rockhampton. The morning was getting on and we all had to be somewhere else. We said our goodbyes and I headed back to the car park; Emu was where I had left him. It wasn't long before I was heading west to Rockhampton looking for the shortcut. I turned right and then right again until I was cruising down a dirt track with some interesting geological scenery and, of course, paddocks dotted with cattle.

I drifted off into my inner world of thoughts, listening to the purr of the engine and the wind blowing through my helmet. Suddenly, a small red ute was beside me, not overtaking just sitting there. Looking over at the driver, I could see he was pointing at something, so I pulled over. He informed me that one of the pannier straps was dangling close to my chain. He was a Harley rider himself (which redeemed all other Harley riders). We talked for some time about motorcycle travel and the places we had been, as I fixed my straps. He said, "Man, it's awesome you're living the dream. Ride safe." In those last words, I knew he understood my journey. I hadn't thought about it until then, but I guess in one way we were all connected through our journeys. Only other bikers know what you're going through and what it feels like to be on the road. I found the shortcut past the caves, as the track curved around a small lava plug from a prehistoric age. I finally came out onto the Bruce Highway, just north of Rockhampton.

Chapter 26
North Queensland's First Deepwater Port

It's hard to believe that one of the earliest registered ports in Queensland with a huge tidal flow was responsible for the economic boom of the late 1800s. I've known of St Lawrence for almost thirty five years, mainly because weather forecasts for Southeast Queensland always span from St. Lawrence to Coolangatta. This always made me curious: Where exactly is St. Lawrence, and why is it so significant?

I enjoy learning history from land markers at rest areas, a hobby that has informed many of the historical references in this book. These markers offer a glimpse into the past and often spark further investigation. I had been riding for almost an hour when I came across a tall granite monument in a rest area dedicated to the region's first miners. It commemorated one of the fastest and least productive gold rushes in Queensland's history, located in a now non-existent place called Canoona. According to the state library, this rush lasted only two months, yet the influx of people from Sydney and Melbourne seeking potential riches significantly contributed to building North Queensland's economy. This was followed by other gold rushes in places like Gympie, Ravenswood,

Charters Towers, and the Palmer River, with many miners from Canoona continuing their quest up the coast.

The inscription on the monument read: "Canoona Gold Field: This stone commemorates the discovery of gold hereabouts by W.C. Chapple in 1857, in the presence of those men who subsequently contributed largely to the establishment of Rockhampton."

I often ponder the early development of towns, especially given the vastness of the Australian landscape. Each town has a reason for its growth, and I am always curious about why and where the people came from. I had never heard of the Canoona Gold Rush before, but it appears to have been a catalyst for Rockhampton's growth and the northward migration of people.

Although I've frequently driven this road, I've rarely stopped to explore the smaller places along the way. Marlborough is one such place. Typically, I would stop there only to refuel or grab a coffee at the highway petrol station, never venturing into the town itself. Today, I decided to explore further. Since it was nearing lunchtime, I looked for a park to set up my cooking gear. Marlborough, was established to support the railway and features a school, a shop, several small businesses, and, of course, a pub.

As I ate, a solitary magpie landed on the table across from me, eyeing my lunch. With a sharp squawk, it hopped toward me and tapped the dish I was holding. As soon as I placed some food on the table, two more magpies joined us. The squawking intensified, and three more birds arrived, making a total of six magpies surrounding me on the table and ground. I tossed bits of food to each before retreating to pack up Emu, my bike. It was like dealing with a Magpie Mafia; these birds were more adept at thievery than even the ducks in Richmond.

The Bruce Highway is shared by grey nomads in their travelling retirement homes, large trucks that rumble past you, creating massive bow waves and surges and the occasional family car or work ute. It's a long hot and dry road with a lot of traffic. There's a well-established rest area at a place called Waverly Creek Rest Area where there are plenty of tables, chairs, and grassed areas to camp if you need to, or in my case, have lunch and a break from riding. It also has a well-maintained toilet facility.

I spent about an hour here, having a coffee and talking with a couple of grey nomads. It was hot on the bike and I needed to remove my riding jacket to cool down. I thought I might be able to find a campsite in St Lawrence so after cooling down I got back on the bike and headed up the road to uncover the mysteries of why the Southeast Queensland weather reports all start from St Lawrence.

St Lawrence was first claimed as a pastoral lease by Europeans in 1859. The town was established as a Customs Office for the Port of St Lawrence. It was the administration centre of the Shire Council of Broadsound until 2008 when it was merged into the Issac Regional Government Area. The town also hosted a meatworks that processed sheep for easier transportation of tallow.

The port benefited from large tidal flows, enabling ships to navigate the estuary and making it one of the deepest ports of its era, ideal for transporting cattle, sheep, and tallow. However, its reliance on this single tidal flow, was not always ideal, and the ever-changing sandbars made navigation hazardous. The port was registered in 1861, the same year the deepwater port at Bowen was discovered, which would eventually become the major port in North Queensland due to its permanent deep-water access. St Lawrence ceased port operations in 1873 after cyclone damage but continued meat processing until 1912.

Some unique geographical features contribute to the weather reporting being taken from St Lawrence. It sits at the junction between Central and North Queensland, making it a good geographical marker of the region. It has several navigational features, including the huge tidal flow and it is still a navigational waterway. The weather report has to be taken from somewhere and St Lawrence is as good a place as any.

I am glad I made the effort to go and have a look at St Lawrence and experience the huge tidal flow. There is more to see here for the tourist and if you want to camp, there is a good little camping ground near the estuary. The camping ground looked fine, but it was a bit exposed; there was very little grass and no shady trees. I wanted to continue a little further up the road and check out a campground at Clairview.

The Clairview Beach Caravan Park is only 20 kilometres further north. When I got there, I was surprised by how good it was and its location. It has very good facilities and ample camping areas for tents, vans, and any other type of camping setup. It even had a restaurant, coffee shop and a bar. The best part was I could pick a quiet out-of-the-way site or pitch my tent overlooking the beach in a long line of tents and vans. Naturally, I took the beach option.

I had initially planned to turn inland at St. Lawrence and follow the Bicentennial Way to Nebo on what would have been a great dirt track. However, given the worn state of my tyres and my growing paranoia about their durability, I decided it would be wiser to continue up the highway. This would conserve my tyres for the final leg of my journey while still allowing me to check out another camping spot. Clairview, about 30 minutes south of Sarina, features several houses overlooking a beach and an expansive mudflat at low tide. There is also a well-maintained, somewhat hidden caravan park with a bar, restaurant, and spacious grassed camping grounds suitable for all types of vehicles and tents.

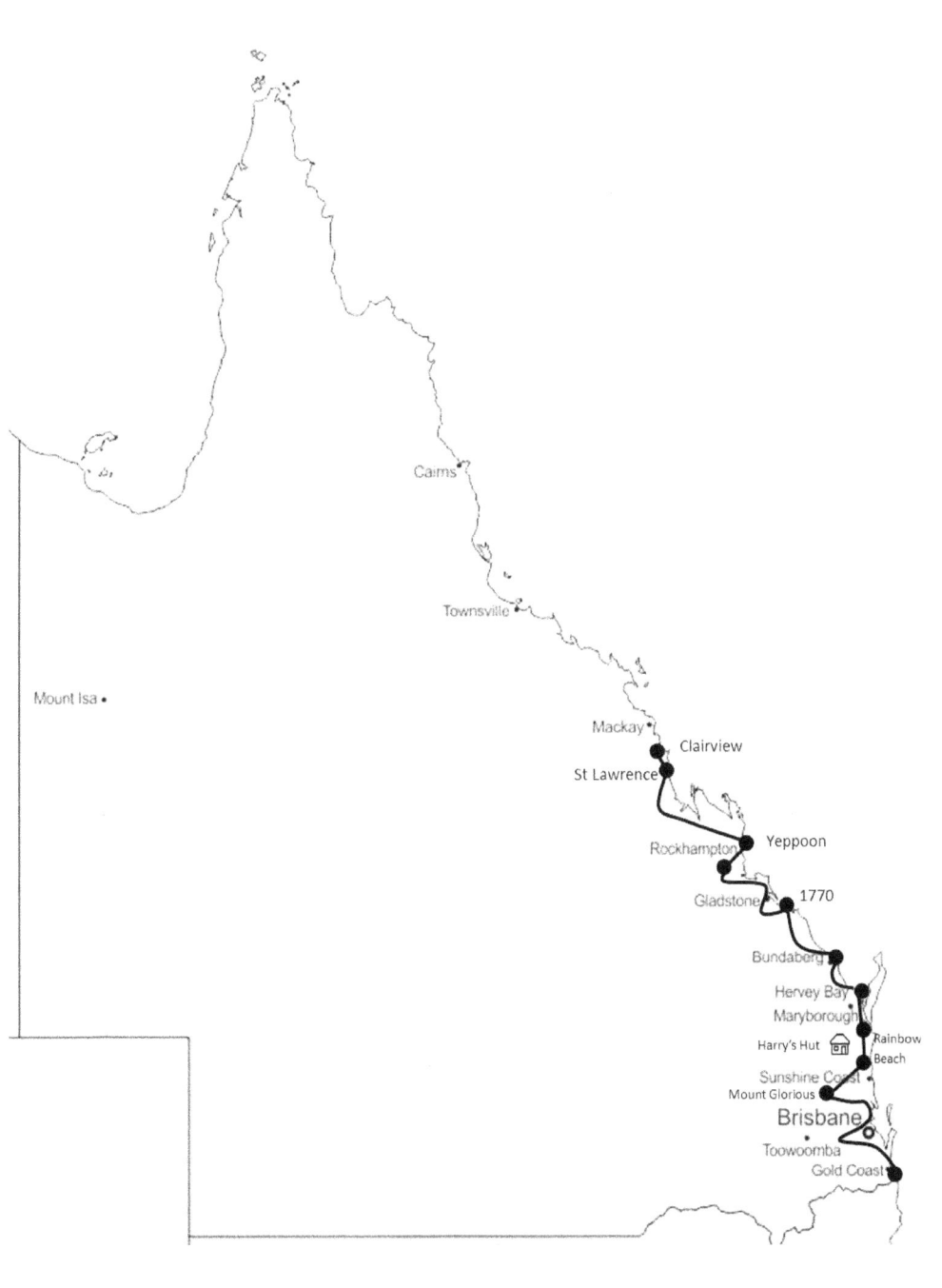

Road to Mount Glorious, Café Racer's dream- Brisbane

Famous Currumbin Rock and the Currumbin Surf Life Saving Club – Gold Coast

Camping near the beach - Maroochydore, Sunshine Coast

Noosa River mouth, one of the biggest tourist areas in Queensland- Noosa, Sunshine Coast

Emu at Harry's Hut, Noosa Everglades - Cooloola Recreational Area

Fellow adventurer, Mike at Harry's Hut - Cooloola Recreational Area

Goanna at Harry's Hut, Noosa Everglades - Cooloola Recreational Area

Monument to Captain Cook's the first landing in Queensland -1770

Waiting for the tide to come in, fishing boats-Yeppoon, Central Queensland

Sunrise over Great Kepple Island-Yeppoon

Monument to the shortest gold rush in Queensland- Central Queensland

Saved, early morning coffee-Yeppoon

Rail Bridge at St Lawrence-Central Queensland

Camping at Clairview-Sarina, Central Queensland

Chapter 27
Back to the Outback

"Life is not about waiting for the storms to pass: it's about learning how to ride in the rain!"
— **Anonymous**

Sitting on my camp chair looking out over the still azure waters of the Barrier Reef Lagoon, I contemplated today's ride. Soon, I would be back on dirt roads, riding through rural properties. There's something uniquely relaxing about riding on dirt—it offers a different adventure compared to the coastal roads. At five in the morning, I was wide awake, coffee in hand, feeling energised and ready for the day ahead.

I had found a site next to a couple who were travelling in their van. We enjoyed a red wine together and they shared their pasta meal with me. The benefits of riding solo are people seem to gravitate to you and it can be easier to start and hold a conversation. I have found the hospitality of fellow travellers generous; you could meet the same people in the middle of the city and not even share eye contact.

It had been windy all night, and for the first time since the campsite overlooking Springsure, I had put all the guy ropes on my tent. The nylon overfly stretches around the tent poles, creating a geometrically strong structure that withstood the night's winds without issue.

The sunrise was a magnificent display of colours and textures as it slowly emerged over the horizon's clouds. Unfortunately, my camera batteries failed just before the sun was fully visible. For anyone camping here, it's well worth waking up early to witness the sunrise. After packing up and saying goodbye to my new friends, I started Emu and prepared for the next part of my adventure. Before heading west to the outback, I needed to refuel. I drove to Sarina, a small sugar refining town about 40 kilometres south of Mackay, filled up, and then turned inland towards Mirani, the gateway to the Pioneer Valley.

My journey today would take me inland from Sarina, through sugarcane fields, and up the winding Clarke Range to Eungella. My goal was to ride through the valley and then hit the dirt road to Eungella Dam, where I hoped to camp for the night.

The road from Sarina to the Pioneer Valley wound through acres of towering cane fields and across numerous train tracks. Since it was "crushing" season, I had to be cautious of the trucks pulling out from the fields without warning and the small cane trains that had the right of way at every crossing. Riding through the cane fields, I often encountered annoying crosswinds, which seemed to come from unpredictable directions. This phenomenon meant that I could never just sit back and enjoy the ride; I always had to stay alert to the wind.

Reaching Mirani, a small support centre at the entrance of the Pioneer Valley, was a relief. While sitting at a table opposite the Mirani Hotel, I watched a cane train loaded with carriages cross the road, holding up traffic for about 10 minutes. The Pioneer

Valley has a rich history, first explored by Europeans in 1860 when a young Scottish man, John Mackay, led an expedition in search of pastoral land. His party crossed over the range and discovered the valley leading to the coastal flats, naming the river after John's father.

However, Commodore Burnett aboard the HMAS *Pioneer* later renamed it the Pioneer River, a decision that angered John Mackay. He lobbied Governor Bowen, who compensated by naming the small town after Mackay instead. Today, the area where John Mackay first descended into the valley is known as Clarke's Range, home to Eungella National Park, the longest continuous sub-tropical rainforest in Australia.

The area soon attracted the emerging sugar industry, thanks to its ample water and flat fertile land, and its future was secured by a global sugar shortage caused by a short civil war in North America.

At the top of the Pioneer Valley is Clarkes Range, which is 690 metres above sea level. My journey up this escarpment went from absolute sea level at Clairview to the lookout overlooking the valley. Once you get to the top, there's a small township called Eungella, an Aboriginal name for land of cloud.

Riding up Clarke's Range is a lot of fun with sharp cambered corners and rising hairpins. Once you get to the top you are rewarded by subtropical rainforest and a cool climate.

On top of the ridge, there are plenty of park benches and tables to enjoy a coffee while looking out over the Pioneer Valley, further down the road drops to the small village of Eungella, which is peaceful and sits on a small creek that is part of the "Broken River" catchment, where if you're quiet you might see a platypus.

There are several camping sites in the Eungella village area just beyond the national park headquarters. Although I was tempted to stay in one of these small and secluded sites, my destination was Eungella Dam for the night. The dam is west of the town and easy to find, as soon as you leave the village the road turns to good even dirt. Follow this for five kilometres and you come across the dam entrance. It's a great place to camp, but before you set up, check the wind direction and camp on the leeward side. It can get quite windy during the night. Just saying.

The dam was built in 1969 to supply water to the mining towns of Collinsville, Scottsville, Glendon, and Moranbah and is managed by Sun Water. Upon arrival, I encountered an unwelcoming sign stating that camping was prohibited for motorcycles, ATVs, and other terrain vehicles. The definition of a terrain vehicle "is any vehicle other than an all-terrain vehicle (ATV)," a motorbike or snowmobile that is designed for and capable of travel over designated unpaved roads. To get here, you have to travel on a designated unpaved road. It means anybody who got here and is reading this sign is not allowed to camp here unless the terrain vehicle is stored on the trailer that the terrain vehicle towed out here. Yeah, not a lot of logic, but that's what happens if you don't go to the doctor immediately to have a stapler removed from your arse. You get infected with gross, illogical thoughts.

As I was on a motorbike that is identified as a prohibited vehicle, I cannot confirm or deny that I camped at this campground and that I may or may not have found a nice little bit of flat ground under the shade of a tree and overlooking the dam. Unfortunately, I was right out of staplers in case the idiot who wrote the sign turned up to inspect my vehicle.

Chapter 28
The Quirkiest Pub in the Outback

I took my time packing up the tent and checking Emu for any loose bolts. Before long, I'm riding down a newly graded road, which makes it fairly fast with a lot of loose gravel in the corners. It's not long before I start going down the western side of Clarkes Range.

The track I'm riding is informally known as the Pipeline Road, or as it is officially known, "The Lizzie Creek Road." This is a well-maintained track used to service the water pipeline from the dam. It dominates the first part of the road, crossing over the road in places.

Riding down the range from Eungella, I come across small valleys with patches of unique flora that is hidden away in protected ecosystems. When I ride through these small ecosystems, I get the feeling I'm in a different part of the world. Trees and bushes vary greatly here from those on the hills and plains that surround these small valleys.

The road eventually flattens out as I get onto the fertile plains. Although I find a slight loss of traction on the small hills due to my worn tires, I manage to maintain a consistent speed of about

70 kilometres per hour. After a hot, breezeless ride lasting two and a half hours, I arrive at the intersection of the Collinsville to Newlands (coal mine) road. You can travel from Collinsville to Nebo via Clermont on the tar-sealed road. However, having driven these roads several times before, I find the rural route far more interesting and exciting. It's about 15 minutes from crossing the Bowen River Bridge to reaching the outskirts of Collinsville.

By the time I got to Collinsville, I was running low on fuel. Collinsville is a mining town. The mines are on the doorstep of the town, so they dominate the landscape. Cattle grazing is also a big industry in this area. Coal mining started in 1912 when full-scale production commenced in Collinsville.

I had spent a lot of time at the dam and I was riding slowly due to the state of my tyres, by the time I got to Collinsville the sun was going down and there were shadows across the road. The road out to the Bowen River Hotel is all dirt but is well-maintained for the 20 kilometres to the hotel. The grading had produced a lot of shingle and sand and with the current state of my tyres, it made for a dangerous ride. With the sun going down, the slippery surface and my fatigue, I had to pay careful attention to my riding and any potential kangaroo that might want to kill me from the side.

Within 30 minutes, I came across the causeway over the Bowen River. The road led steeply uphill to the historic Bowen River Hotel. The Bowen River may look peaceful and inviting, but it's full of saltwater crocodiles. I have seen photos of five-metre crocodiles in the river. It is estimated that estuarine or saltwater crocodiles inhabit the river up to where the Bowen River meets the Broken River. This is approximately 225 kilometres from the coast and another 100 kilometres further from where I am now. It just goes to show you can't take for granted the absence of crocodiles in North Queensland, even in freshwater inland rivers.

At the heritage-listed Bowen River Hotel, there's a hitching post where I metaphorically hitched Emu. I headed into the bar and asked if I could camp out back. The hotel, which hosts events like rodeos and farming workshops and offers mining-type accommodations, has ample camping space. I paid ten dollars to pitch my tent on a grassy area near the toilet and shower facilities, set up my tent, and enjoyed a hot shower. Emu was parked on the grassy campsite next to my tent, covered with his camouflage tarp to protect against the night's dew. As the temperature began to drop, I was grateful to have my down jacket once more.

There is some confusion regarding the actual history of the Bowen River Hotel. It is believed to have originally been called the Heidelberg Inn, built in 1865. This was shortly after the nearby town of Bowen was discovered by Europeans in 1859 and settled in 1861. There is uncertainty about whether the current Bowen River Hotel was once the Heidelberg Inn. In the same area, there were two hotels: the Heidelberg Inn and the Bowen River Hotel, referred to as the upper and lower hotels, respectively. The upper was known as the Heidelberg Inn and the lower as the Bowen River Hotel. Records are scarce, but it is known that after a severe rainstorm one wet season, only one hotel remained. Since there is no ground higher than where the current hotel stands, the mystery continues.

Considering the amount of water that flows down the Bowen River during the wet season, it wouldn't be hard to imagine anything lower than the current hotel being swept away.

After exploring the grounds, setting up my camp, and partaking in a few red wines, I went to the bar to order food. There were two items available that night, a steak sandwich and a Chicken Parmigiana. As several locals had rocked up for a birthday celebration, I quickly decided on the Chicken Parmigiana.

On a sign at the entry to this pub is a historical marker stating: "On this exact spot at 6:45 on the afternoon of April 27th, 1958. A marital argument was had and won by the husband." Secretly anonymous – Bowen River Hotel Patron

Whether fact or fiction, opinions vary. Some find it unbelievable, while others feel sorry for the husband, knowing the consequences that would surely follow. This all happened at the Bowen River Hotel, 20 kilometres west of the mining town of Collinsville.

Suddenly, Toyota utes with high-powered spotlights, dogs in cages, and rifles on the bench seats filled the area. The front of the pub quickly became crowded with work vehicles, turning into a vibrant party. I sat to the side, enjoying my red wine and parmigiana, soaking in the ambiance. The pub has been a hub for both travellers and locals for over 156 years. I retreated for a restful night, anticipating an early rise to watch the sunrise.

Chapter 29
Gold Fever

"The road never ends ... only our vision does."
— **Amit Reddy**

As usual, I rise early, but before brewing my morning coffee, I grab my camera and head down to the Bowen River causeway. The sky is a dark blue crimson with a hint of light blue over the distant eastern ranges. Hoping to spot a crocodile on the river's sandbanks, I tread quietly down the steep hill to the causeway.

It's the most peaceful time of the day, with cool air and birds just beginning to stir. Standing on the causeway, I gaze down the river, wondering about the presence of crocodiles below. The elusive nature of crocodiles means you can never be sure of their whereabouts.

The first part of my ride today is along a rural access road to the back of the Burdekin Dam. It's the last time on this trip that I will ride a dirt road, and I'm somewhat sad that my journey is nearing its end. However, I've pledged to do more adventure riding and have realised that there's much more to explore in Queensland. When I get home, I'll be updating my bucket list.

There were no crocodiles in sight. By the time I returned to my camp, I was in dire need of coffee and desperately searched through my side panniers to retrieve the stove and avoid my imminent collapse from caffeine withdrawal. The sun was beginning to light up the sky, its another crystal-clear morning, the dark inky sky fading into a bright blue pierced by rays of golden light.

Breakfast consisted of a couple of cups of coffee, muesli, and a cheese and biscuit snack pack. I was unsure of my next destination, but I had chatted with some locals last night who assured me that the turn-off was just up the road, about half an hour away, and hard to miss. Buoyed by their directions and my new GPS, I finished my breakfast, packed my gear, and set out to explore the outback once more.

My journey today would take me deeper into this rural landscape and I would travel the route taken by miners and swaggies back in the late 1800s. No sooner had I crossed the first creek than I noticed how bad my tyres were. Pulling out of the sand and accelerating up the hill, I could feel the back end sliding and skipping. There was very little traction. The only thing I could do was keep the throttle open in the hope that shear tyre rotation would get me up the other side.

I continued up and down the gears, sliding on the steeper sections while all the time looking out for the left turn that would take me to the Burdekin Dam. The 30 minutes to the turnoff had come and gone. I continued riding, believing it would appear any moment now. It has been well over an hour and my advice had been that it would take two hours to get to the dam. The turn-off should be any time now, or had I inadvertently missed it?

Refusing to believe I had been so inattentive as to head toward a remote corner of the outback in the opposite direction of my destination, I was startled when two huge kangaroos jumped out just in front of me. If I had been going faster, I might have hit them. Taking this as a sign, I reminded myself to pay closer attention.

After about an hour and a half, I came to a junction. The signpost indicated Mount Elise to the left and Glenroy Station to the right, with no mention of Burdekin Dam. Thinking to rely on my GPS, I punched in "Burdekin Dam" only for it to die on me. Each attempt to calculate the route resulted in it shutting down.

I took the left road for about five minutes until I came across another sign that indicated "Pyramid" and "Hidden Valley." These locations were marked on my map but were clearly in the wrong direction, so I turned around and headed back to the fork in the road.

My paper map indicated that Glenroy Station was generally in the direction of the dam, but it didn't show a connecting road between the two. Concerned that I might have missed the actual turn-off, I decided to turn around and ride slowly back to see if I could locate it.

After about two minutes, a Toyota Land Cruiser approached from the opposite direction, carrying a young man and woman. They stopped to ask if I needed any help. He had a CRF250 strapped to the back and mentioned he was checking fence lines in the area.

We chatted about bikes for about ten minutes. When I inquired about the turn-off to the Burdekin Dam, he advised me to follow the Glenroy Station Road. I thanked him, and we went our separate ways. When I reached the turn-off, I took the right bend and entered a more hilly and sandy part of the track.

The road to the dam was quite different from the access road I had been on for the past hour and a half. Although well-maintained, this road had steep uphill sections and correspondingly downhill stretches, each ending in a sweeping sandy corner. This would be fine on a light dirt bike or even on an adventure bike with good tires, but it was challenging on a heavy adventure bike with bald tyres.

On more than one occasion, the back tyre would just skip halfway and I doubted I would get up the hill. This had nothing to do with horsepower; I simply lost traction. Going down the other side was equally harrowing as there was very little control coming into the corners. Finally, I crested one of the steeper hills and saw the Burdekin Dam laid out in front of me. It was a mix of relief and sadness, knowing it marked the end of my dirt road adventure for now.

Riding over the last hill, I was struck by the sight of the magnificent Burdekin Dam and its concrete spillway below—a real "wow" moment. The transition from slippery dirt to smooth tar was a relief, yet the view of such an impressive structure was overwhelming.

The Burdekin Dam Spillway is a formidable piece of infrastructure. The road crosses at the base of the spillway, which is closed when the dam overflows. As I rode down the steep, winding road to the concrete access road, I felt tiny compared to the giant concrete mass. To my right, the mighty Burdekin River ran through a vast gorge that looked to be made of ironstone, over 800 metres wide and 40 metres deep.

The road was steep and narrow, curling around the side of an almost sheer cliff, thankfully all tar-sealed. I later found out that the dam had recorded over 10 metres of overflow above the spillway.

The sheer force of that sort of water over a road or bridge would surely destroy it. The heat had suddenly risen and the sun was reflecting off thousands of tonnes of concrete.

Constant water discharge from the dam ensures that sugar farmers in the Burdekin Valley can irrigate their crops. But what I wasn't expecting to find was a family of pelicans thriving in this little turbulent ecosystem at the bottom of the Burdekin Dam Spillway.

The Burdekin Dam is called the Burdekin Falls Dam, construction was started in 1984 and completed by 1987. The first time it filled was in 1988 during the wet season. The catchment is called Lake Dalrymple, which can hold up to 1,860,000 mega litres of water. It cost 125 million dollars to build.

Once I ride out of the gorge, there's a caravan park on top of the hill overlooking the spillway. There's nowhere in the village to stop and make a coffee or have lunch, but as you leave there's a boat ramp with plenty of tables and a toilet facility.

I decided to stop here for a short break before riding the 75 kilometres to Ravenswood. The dam looks inviting but I have seen a video by a fisherman of a saltwater crocodile at least four metres long on the banks. So, swim at your own risk.

As I was boiling my billy, a small, obviously young magpie decided to join me. He was a friendly fellow so I shared a couple of morsels of my muesli bar. But it appears this little bird was the fall guy for a well-rehearsed organised crime syndicate. No sooner had he hopped away with his reward than I was surrounded by a gang of terrorising mature magpies.

Not only did I have to contend with magpies on the table and dancing around my feet, but I had to be vigilant of the aerial assault as well. After defending my food for a good 30 minutes, I threw some muesli bar pieces at one magpie who was the point bird. This made him the target of aggression for the other more senior magpies. As they squabbled over the pieces, I packed up and made a quick getaway.

The road between the Burdekin Falls Dam and the town of Ravenswood runs along a ridge line. I tried to imagine what it must have been like in 1867 with miners and swaggies walking along the ridge during the summer. It takes about 45 minutes at highway speed to get to Ravenswood. By the time I arrived, it was well after lunchtime. I pulled up at the Imperial Hotel to see if I could get a bite to eat in an attempt to reduce the chances of another mugging by organised crime magpies.

Two hotels remain in Ravenswood, the Imperial Hotel and the Railway Hotel, and they're great examples of late 19th-century classical architecture.

After a large burger, chips, and salad, I got on Emu and went to the council camping ground. There are two camping grounds in Ravenswood, Top Park at the northern entrance and Council Park opposite the multi-denominational church, which was once the Catholic Church.

I stayed in the council camping ground at Ravenswood. It was a warmish night but for some reason I didn't get a lot of sleep. I'm up early boiling my billy and contemplating what this place must have been like in its heyday. The town is a virtual living museum, the buildings are all late 1800s. There are examples of steam engines and pumps laying around all over the place.

When the first miners came to this area, there were no roads or tracks just grassland, creek beds, and these funny white silica rocks with yellow flex of gold in them. Then, "Eureka!" If I close my eyes, I can feel the excitement, I can hear and see the exhalation, a mixture of relief and sheer joy that one gets when the difficulties of life seem to fade away as the realisation that a more comfortable life is just around the corner, all thanks to that little spec of yellow metal, gold.

These must have been the words of the Curr Brothers while prospecting on Conolly Creek on a hot and humid day in 1868 at Merri Merriiwa Station. How do I assume it was hot and humid? Simple deductive reasoning: north Queensland experiences hot and humid conditions about 80% of the year; otherwise, it's just plain hot.

Interestingly, at the same time, Thomas Aitken was jumping up and down after discovering gold on the neighbouring Ravenswood Station. Both the Curr Brothers and Aitken initially had more interest in land for cattle grazing than gold mining. Thomas Aitken eventually took his find to the new port of Townsville and purchased land south of the port, now known as Aitkenvale.

The gold rush began in earnest in 1869 with the discovery of major gold reefs in Nolan's, Jessop, and Buchanan gullies on the southern side of Elphinstone Creek. Two camps, Upper and Lower Camps, were set up, with Upper Camp eventually becoming the Ravenswood township. Three mining pits were developed: "General Grant" (named after the Union general during the American Civil War, which had just ended), Sunset, and eventually Sarsfield.

Transport routes were quickly established from Bowen, the only deep-water port in Queensland at the time. The route passed the Boggie River, a newly opened pub called the Bowen Hotel, crossed the river where the Burdekin Dam now stands, and followed the ridge to Ravenswood Station—the very route I rode yesterday.

The town is still a gold mining town and a new open cut is operating near the graveyard.

I realise that I've just done an amazing big loop of Queensland. I started with gold in Charters Towers and I'm ending with gold in Ravenswood only 50 kilometres apart.

This is my last ride on my 30-day adventure around Queensland. I'm riding home to Townsville. On one hand, I'm sad that it's ending; on the other, I'm proud of myself for taking up the challenge of riding around Queensland solo on a motorcycle.

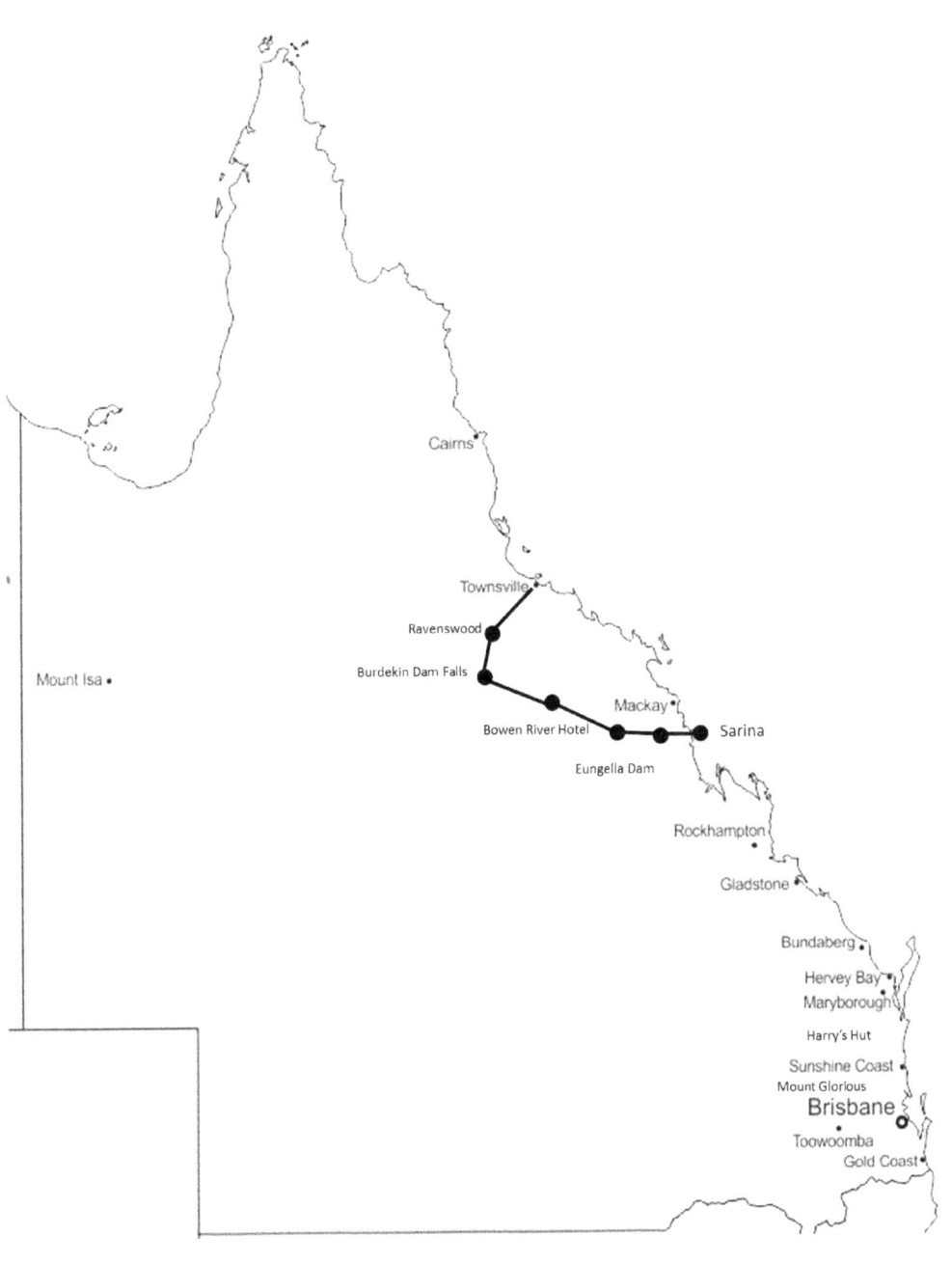

Pioneer Valley - Mackay

Cane Train-Marani

No adventure bikes allowed, Eungella Dam

The last dirt track ends just above the Burdekin Dam – North Queensland

Hitching post at the Bowen River Hotel – Collinsville

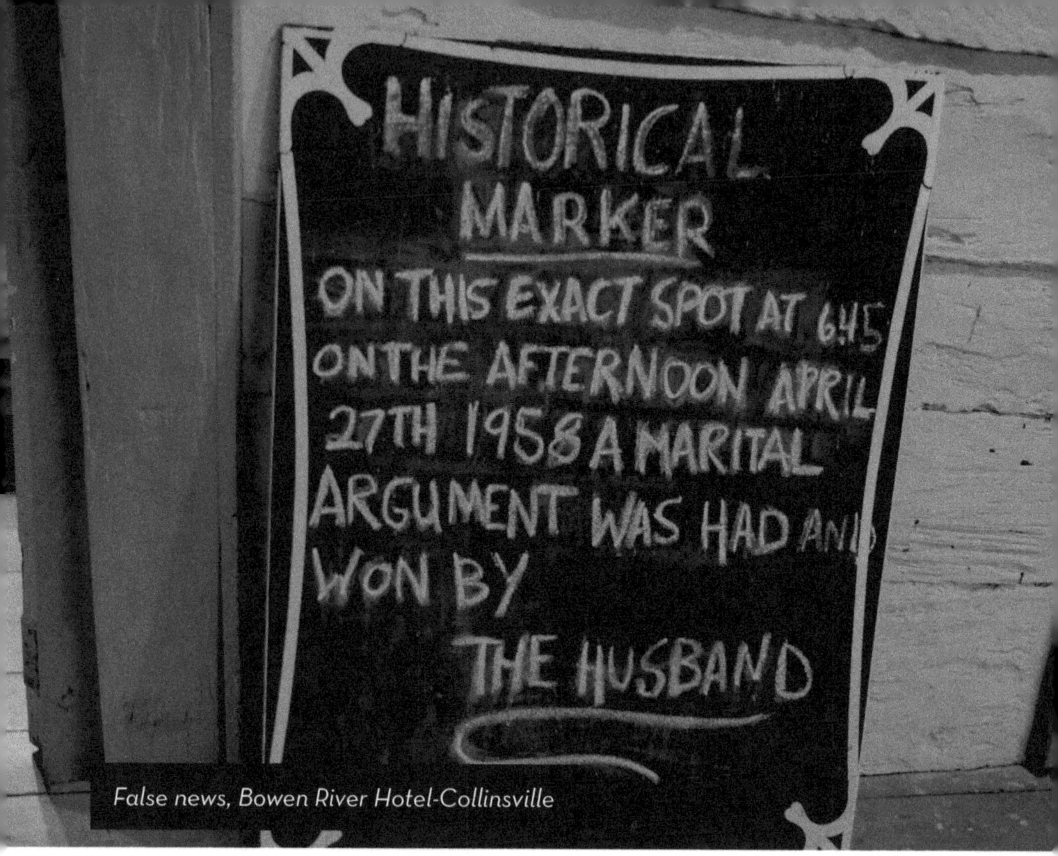
HISTORICAL
MARKER
ON THIS EXACT SPOT AT 6.45
ON THE AFTERNOON APRIL
27TH 1958 A MARITAL
ARGUMENT WAS HAD AND
WON BY
THE HUSBAND

False news, Bowen River Hotel-Collinsville

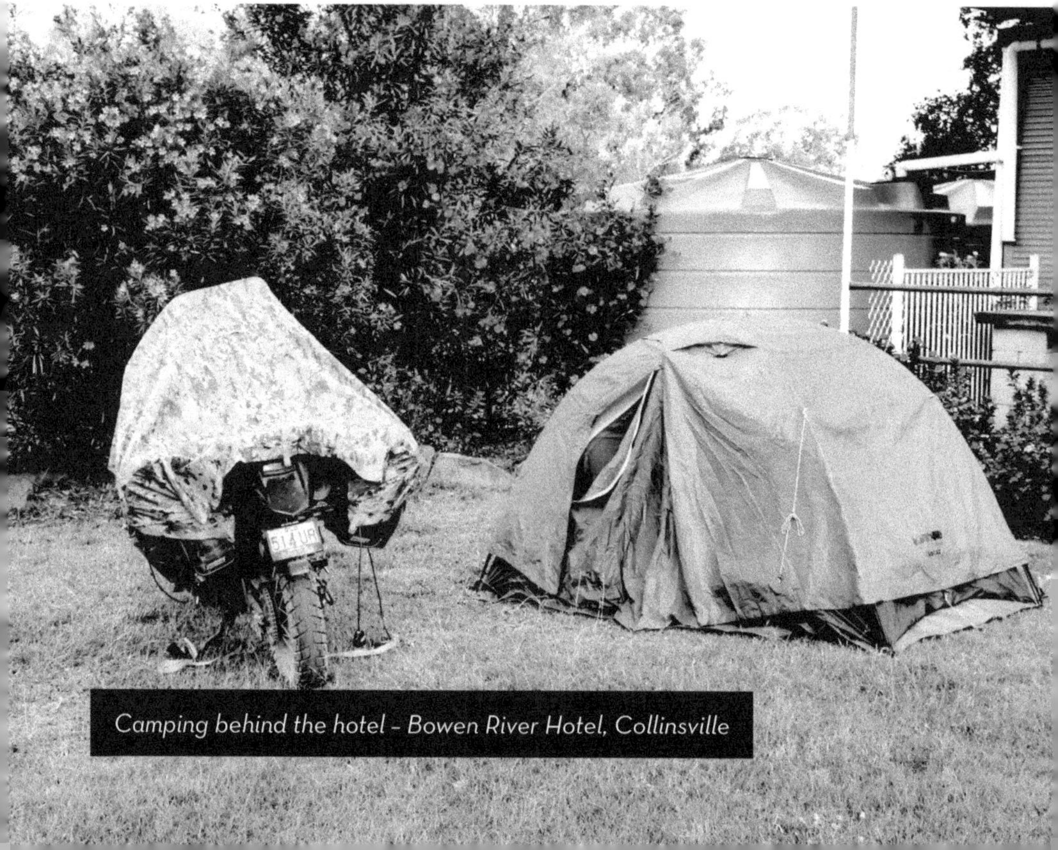
514 UR

Camping behind the hotel – Bowen River Hotel, Collinsville

Bowen River Hotel, early morning - Collinsville

Pelican Family, Burdekin Dam - North Queensland

Spillway, Burdekin Dam - North Queensland

Lunch at the Burdekin Dam, watch out for lunch bandits-Ravenswood

Emu outside the Imperial Hotel-Ravenswood

Chapter 30
Back in Townsville

"The purpose of life, after all, is to live it, to taste experience to the utmost, to reach out eagerly and without fear for a newer and richer experience."

— **Eleanor Roosevelt**

My adventure around Queensland has accumulated close to 8,000 kilometres of adventure touring on my KLR650. In approximately one and a half hours, I will turn left, corner hard on a roundabout, and drive up a short driveway to my home in Townsville.

I didn't go to every town in Queensland, so now I'm feeling like there's some unfinished business. I did cover a fair amount of ground, from the dusty outback roads to Opalton to the sandstone cliffs of Carnarvon Gorge. Eventually, I made it to the clear blue azure waters of the Pacific Ocean. Mind you, looking at it on the map, it still looks like I have a lot further to go and a lot more to see. Queensland is immense—both the United Kingdom and New Zealand could fit within its borders. It's as varied as any country in terms of culture, scenery, and landscape.

I couldn't help but make some observations about our society as I rode through countless small towns and down the arterial roads that are the lifeblood of this state.

There's a dichotomy in Queensland's culture, separated by the Great Dividing Range. On one side, there's a community with strong Australian values of hard work, honesty, integrity, and mateship, complete with chicken races and teddy bears. There's always a friendly face, a welcoming smile, and a curious "G'day, mate, where've you come from?" It's a place where people acknowledge each other with a finger raise or a nod.

On the other side, there's a more "woke" culture—fast-paced, frantic, and commercialised, favouring individualism. Here, the pursuit of financial independence and career progression or entrepreneurship is the norm. In this world, nobody looks up, nobody acknowledges you, and cars race by at high speeds, burning large amounts of fossil fuel to quickly reach the next traffic jam. It's easy to get caught up in this world, thinking it's the only way.

It looks like a new religion is in town, "Environmental Liberalism" with its wrathful god, "Climate Change." This new religion has replaced the traditional Christian faith of the past 2,000 years. Interestingly, there is this great green movement in our cities, but having just travelled through the outback, I can't help feeling there's no place less green than cities. Riding a motorcycle around Queensland, I tried to stop at almost every beach, to find the "best" one, an elusive dream. They're all great, albeit some are greater than others.

In my short tour of Queensland, I have learnt not to worry about the small things, as Mark Manson states in his book *The Subtle Art of Not Giving a F&ck:* "Looking for only positive experiences is in itself a negative experience and paradoxically the acceptance of one's negative experience is itself a positive experience."

What does this have to do with motorcycle touring? It's simply this: When you ride a motorcycle, shit happens. It rains, you get a flat tyre, some idiot almost kills you, your chain breaks, your battery dies, and kangaroos have no common sense (that last one is not a thing, just an observation). You don't need to worry about those things. You'll deal with them and they'll make you more positive and resilient in the long run. Phrases like "shit happens" and "If it doesn't kill you, it makes you stronger" are all coined to help you not give a fuck.

What has become obvious to me, is that to get to your destination, you have to fix the immediate problem that presents itself and move on. It's pure self-reliance. But as a solo traveller, moving on can be anytime you make it. You're not on the clock. When you get where you're going, your experiences are overwhelmingly positive. You've made it. I have found two types of things that helped me balance negative emotions, "wow" factors, and "moments". The more of these I have, the better my experience and the more positive I feel.

Some people might say, "So what?" You rode a motorcycle around Queensland for a month, it's not the long way round, it's not Ted Simon's four-year adventure around the world or Chris Donaldson's tour of war-torn Africa. They are right, but who says an adventure must be an epic journey to be meaningful? Can I ride through Africa or India? You bet I can. They all start with a well-maintained bike, camping gear, and the twist of the throttle.

I now know what Curley meant when he held up his finger in that immortal gesture to Billy Crystal in the movie, *City*

Slickers. I think that one thing is different for everyone. For me, it represents freedom. Not in the way of being completely unshackled and living a stress-free hippy life, but freedom of the mind and knowing if I can ride a motorcycle around Queensland, I can ride it anywhere. It is freedom to move beyond my current mindset to explore new possibilities.

Take this into your everyday life and you realise the only person you need to be happy, is yourself. And what better way of doing it than by riding a motorcycle around Queensland?

This morning, as I woke up in an overwhelmingly positive mood, I was almost at the end of my first major motorcycle adventure. I should have been sad, but I wasn't because I had achieved three bucket list items. These included finding an opal at Opalton, writing a story about the poor old swaggie that got murdered at the Combo Waterhole, and riding a motorcycle around Queensland.

My tour included camping in out-of-the-way places, marvelling at the sheer beauty of nature, and meeting interesting people, just like a modern-day swaggie.

This older guy walked up to me as I sat waiting for my billy to boil next to my tent and contemplating this story. "Giday, mate, where you from?" he said. I smiled; I was back on the right side of the line. In my mind, riding a motorcycle around Queensland is a large undertaking, each day is an epic adventure.

One of the most satisfying things I did when riding a motorcycle around Queensland was pack my bike. At the end of the packing process, I was ready to roll onto the next adventure.

This morning was the last time I would pack up my kit on this trip. I followed the same routine I had maintained over the past month: packing slowly, ensuring everything was in its place, then performing the regular bike checks. I checked the oil levels, cleaned and lubricated the chain, and ensured the panniers and packs were securely stowed. After donning my jacket, helmet, glasses, and gloves, and putting the keys in the ignition, I was set to go. Apart from a fuel stop about halfway home, this would be the last time on this trip that I would go through this procedure.

Pressing the starter, Emu comes to life. The quiet "pop, pop, pop" of the big 650 single engine is comforting, like the purring of a family cat. I let him rev under choke for a few minutes. Then, placing my foot on the peg, I pivot around, making sure my leg swings above my pack on the back of the seat, like a cowboy mounting his steed. It's a reassuring feeling, perched between my pack and my tank bag.

Looking up at the horseshoe-shaped dirt road that feeds campers and caravans into this park, I notice dogs are being taken for a walk and a couple of small kids are playing with a football. As I ride out, I can't resist standing on the pegs and sharply twisting the throttle. The engine revs as I lean slightly to the right, causing the back wheel to slide out to the left. Keeping the revs up, I lean to the centre and turn the front wheel in the direction I want to go.

Executing a perfect power slide, I sit down and straighten up, allowing Emu to pull out of the slide and rocket forward. I cruise through Ravenswood, out to Mingela, and onto the highway east to Townsville. After refuelling halfway down the range, it's not long before the outer areas of Townsville come into view. I pass the army base before reaching the turn-off that will take me home. Soon, I will turn left, corner hard on a roundabout, and drive up a short driveway to my home. I'm back, but I'm not the same person who left. I've become more self-reliant, less concerned about the small things in life, and more focused on what truly matters—continuing my adventurous lifestyle. The pursuit of an upwardly mobile life no longer appeals to me. Strangely, very few people ask me about my trip, not even my family. Sometimes I wonder if we are all too caught up in our new servant reality.

Now, sitting back in my hammock, I've cleaned the mud and dirt from Emu and cleaned and stored my camping gear. Sipping on a glass of red wine as the sky darkens and the road noise from the highway softens, I play "Dock of the Bay" on my speaker. Listening to the melodic music, I raise one finger in the air. This is unfinished business. I think I need to ride to Cape York.

www.ingramcontent.com/pod-product-compliance
Lightning Source LLC
Chambersburg PA
CBHW042320090526
44585CB00024BA/2654